SWEET HEAT

Spicy Desserts (& More!) for Chile Lovers

Melissa T. Stock & Dave DeWitt

PHOTOGRAPHS BY
Lois Ellen Frank

TEN SPEED PRESS
Berkeley, California

🔟

Ten Speed Press

Box 7123

Berkeley, California 94707

Distributed in Australia by E.J. Dwyer Pty. Ltd., in Canada by
Publishers Group West, in New Zealand by Tandem Press, in South Africa
by Real Books, and in the United Kingdom and Europe by Airlift Books.

Cover and text design by Nancy Austin.

Cover photograph and interior photographs by Lois Ellen Frank, Santa Fe.

Library of Congress Cataloging-in-Publication Data

Stock, Melissa T.

Sweet heat/Melissa T. Stock and Dave DeWitt; photography by
Lois Ellen Frank.

    p.   cm.

Includes bibliographical references and index.

ISBN 0-89815-817-6

    1. Cookery (Hot peppers)   2. Hot peppers.   3. Confectionery.

I. DeWitt, Dave   II. Title

TX803.P46S76   1996

641.6'384—dc20

                                     95-50767

                                     CIP

First printing, 1996

Printed in Canada

1 2 3 4 5 6 7 8 9 10 — 00 99 98 97 96

This book
is lovingly dedicated to
Dan Stock and Mary Jane Wilan.
And to Grandma Pearl,
my Kitchen Angel.

CONTENTS

▲▲▲▲▲▲▲▲▲▲▲▲▲▲▲▲▲▲▲▲▲▲▲▲▲▲▲▲▲▲▲▲▲▲▲▲▲▲▲

ACKNOWLEDGMENTS

▲▲

We cannot imagine creating a book without the input and taste buds of our many helpful friends. Thanks to all the lovers of the sweet and the heat who helped with this project: Claude Barthé, Jeff Campbell, Roxanne E. Chan, Jeff Corydon, John Philips Cranwell, Suzy Dayton, Jasmine DeLuisa, Robert Dixon, Stella Fong, Nancy Gerlach, Nancy Austin, Lorena Jones, Arnold Krochmal, James B. O'Malley, Lynn Moretti, David Paul, Philip Podovani, Lynda Pozel, Irene Day Randall, Kathy Redford, Marilou Robinson, Mrs. Leonard Shugart, Robert Spiegel, Dan Stock, Dorothy Stock, Susana Trilling, Robb Walsh, Tamilyn Wedlow, Mary Jane Wilan, and Peter Zimmer.

And most special thanks to our hot helpers on the *Chile Pepper* staff: Sheila Adams, Connie Bleiweis, Debbie Beldring, Cathleen Chamness, and Ilene Style.

Finally, a huge thank you to three swell gals, Lois Berthold, Kellye Hunter, Cathleen Karczewski, and Denice Skrepcinski, who maintained their good humor while assisting us with baking the treats for this book.

INTRODUCTION

▲▲▲▲▲▲▲▲▲▲▲▲▲▲▲▲▲▲▲▲▲▲▲▲▲▲▲▲▲▲▲▲▲▲▲▲▲▲▲

Sweet Heat is a natural part of the entire fiery foods movement. All over the country, people are adding chiles to everything from their morning coffee to their tofu salads for lunch, so why not sweets?

We didn't invent the concept, but this is the first book completely devoted to pairing sweet things with chile heat. Actually, the combination of chiles and sweets goes back to the Mayans, who flavored their hot chocolate with fiery chiles and honey. These days, this idea has been expanded greatly, as many types of chiles are added to every food imaginable.

In fact, the trend of hot desserts is becoming more mainstream every day; Lifesavers Candies has produced a hot and spicy flavor, and the Stonewall Chili Pepper Company has created habanero citrus drops. There are jalapeño suckers, hot gummy chiles, and even chocolate-covered red chile cherries.

We do know a bit about things hot and spicy, being the editor-in-chief and managing editor of *Chile Pepper* magazine, respectively. Besides both being cooks and writers, between us we have accumulated more than 14 years of chile knowledge and written more than 15 books on the subject.

This is very clearly a book devoted to indulgences. *Sweet Heat* presents plenty of opportunities to indulge a double addiction—to chiles and sugar—and not to mention other sinful delights such as chocolate and mangoes. Although we *have* placed at least one lower-in-fat recipe in each chapter, it has been impossible to eliminate all of the fat and sugar in these recipes. We do not suggest substituting artificial sweeteners in any baked recipe in this book, although they may be used in drinks and fruit desserts.

In this book we've covered dangerous drinks, and chile-spiked sauces, well-spiced creams, sorbets, and even breads and cookies. Pies and cakes are represented in full force, as are candies, custards, fruits, jellies, and jams. We've included our favorite recipes, collected from near and far, from childhood memories, chefs, and our personal creations, and collections. We have combined them with our baking experiences, tips and hints, anecdotes, facts, and tidbits about the desserts.

One tip—perhaps the most important one—applies to all the recipes in this book and should always be observed when working with chiles: be careful not to touch your eyes, nose, or any other part of your body when handling fresh or dried chiles. Wash your hands with soap and water immediately after preparing chiles. If they still burn or feel "hot," wash them in milk. Or, if you want to play it safe, simply wear plastic gloves when peeling or chopping chiles, but, remember, don't touch those eyes!

Finally, a note on the heat scale we've included in the book. We've used the same mild, medium, hot, and extremely hot ratings for the recipes that run in the magazine. They are based on our own tastes, taking into consideration the type of chile used in the recipe, as well as the amount called for. We have also included mail-order sources in the back of the book for chiles that may be difficult to obtain in some parts of the country.

Feel free to adjust the heat in these desserts up or down according to your own taste. But whatever you do, remember, life is short so eat dessert first!

1

INCANDESCENT CANDIES

Candy has been one of the most tantalizing treats throughout the centuries! The story of candy begins with honey, a main source of sweetness in much of the world. For, even the folks from the Stone Age were known to raid a beehive or two looking for something a little sweet. And of course the Egyptians, never a people to miss out on anything good, were dipping nuts into honey by 1560 BC.

Around 3000 BC, sugar was made into sugarcane sap in India. Nougat was also discovered in India during this time. By 700 AD, Arab countries were receiving this precious cargo by way of traders, along with the secrets on how to turn the sugarcane into sugar. Not long after that, cane shoots and the knowledge of what to do with them crossed the Mediterranean, and in short order, candy-making arrived in Italy and France.

In the Middle Ages, candy was only available to the very rich. However, by the fifteenth century it was more common, and the astrologer Nostradamus was so taken by the art of candy-making that he wrote a book, *The French Confectioner*, about the subject. Sugar became accessible to most people by the Renaissance. Columbus took sugarcane to the West Indies where it quickly became a major crop to meet the growing demands of Europe. Penny candy was available in Europe by the seventeenth century.

We offer these recipes with just one caveat: they cannot be doubled. If you wish to make additional candies, always whip up separate batches.

And now begin a sweet hot journey with a composium of spicy candies that both Nostradamus and Columbus would covet.

GRAND CAYENNE
GOOD-GOODS

Yield: 32

Heat Scale: Medium

Bon bons, the official name of this confection, translates from French to "good goods." You'll find this is the tastiest treat by any name; it's the perfect gift for your sweetheart on Valentine's Day or any other occasion. Note: This recipe requires some advance preparation.

2 cups creme-filled chocolate cookie crumbs

$^1/_2$ cup confectioners' sugar

2 teaspoons cayenne powder

2 tablespoons unsweetened cocoa

2 tablespoons light corn syrup

$^1/_3$ cup Grand Marnier liqueur

1 cup chopped walnuts

3 tablespoons granulated sugar

6 ounces semisweet or white chocolate, melted

In a medium bowl, combine the cookie crumbs, confectioners' sugar, cayenne powder, cocoa, corn syrup, liqueur, and walnuts. Blend the mixture well, then cover with plastic wrap and refrigerate for 1 hour or longer. Shape the dough into 1-inch balls, and roll in granulated sugar. Store in airtight container for at least 1 day.

Line a baking sheet with waxed paper. Dip half of each ball in melted chocolate; place $^1/_2$ inch apart on a prepared baking sheet. Refrigerate until firm. Store covered in the refrigerator.

ALMOST TRADITIONAL
PEANUT BUTTER CUPS

Yield: 16

Heat Scale: Medium

These look like the real thing, but have that secret ingredient that we all love so much! New Mexican red chile complements the earthy taste of peanut butter with a sweet addition of chocolate. These are also incredible when crumbled and used as a topping on the Pear and Pasilla-Caramel Ice Cream (page 182).

2 cups semisweet chocolate chips

1 cup milk chocolate chips

2 tablespoons butter

1 cup creamy peanut butter

2 teaspoons New Mexican red chile powder

16 paper baking cups

Combine the chocolate chips and butter in a microwave-safe bowl and microwave on 50-percent power for 1 minute. Remove and stir, continuing to cook on 50-percent power for 20-second intervals until the chocolate is well blended and smooth. Set aside.

In a double boiler, combine the peanut butter and chile. Melt the peanut butter, stirring until smooth and set aside. Next, line up the cupcake wrappers on a cookie sheet. Place 1 tablespoon of melted chocolate into each of the baking cups, then let them cool.

When the chocolate is cool, place 1 tablespoon of the melted peanut butter chile mixture into each of the baking cups. Let cool thoroughly.

Finally, place 1 tablespoon of the melted chocolate chile mixture over each peanut butter layer in the baking cups. Let the candies cool completely and store in the refrigerator.

HABANERO TRUFFLES

Yield: About 36

Heat Scale: Hot

🔥 🔥 🔥

Melissa first experienced this candy on a Caribbean cruise. She tasted it on the island of Antigua where she toured rum distilleries and beautiful beaches. You may roll these truffles in chopped nuts of your choice if you're not a coconut fan.

2 cups milk chocolate chips

$^1/_3$ cup butter

$^1/_2$ teaspoon habanero powder

$^1/_4$ cup half-and-half

1 tablespoon rum

$^1/_4$ cup minced mango

Flaked coconut

Combine the chocolate chips, butter, habanero powder, and half-and-half in a microwave-safe bowl and microwave on 50-percent power for 1 minute. Remove, stir, and continue to cook on 50-percent power in 30-second increments until the chocolate is smooth and well blended. Stir in the rum and mango. Place the mixture in the refrigerator and chill for about 15 minutes.

When the mixture is almost hard, drop the candy by teaspoonful into the coconut. Shape the candies into 1-inch balls with your fingers.

BANANA JALAPEÑO FONDANT

Yield: 40
Heat Scale: Medium

This tropical candy teams banana extract and the quick heat of jalapeños for a confectionery creation that's sure to please. This recipe is adaptable to any whim you may have; try adding food coloring to the mixture for some colorful candy, or try cherry extract instead of banana.

$4^{1}/_{2}$ cups sifted confectioners' sugar

$^{1}/_{3}$ cup butter

1 teaspoon jalapeño powder

$^{1}/_{2}$ cup light corn syrup

1 teaspoon vanilla extract

1 teaspoon banana extract

Yellow food coloring (optional)

Combine 2 cups of the sugar, along with the butter, jalapeño powder, and corn syrup in a heavy saucepan and cook over low heat, stirring constantly, until the mixture comes to a boil. Quickly add the remaining sugar and vanilla and stir. Remove from the heat.

Continue to stir the mixture in the saucepan until it holds its shape. Pour the candy into a greased bowl. Let the mixture cool until it is cool enough to be handled. Knead the mixture until it is smooth, then mix in the banana extract. Add the food coloring. Shape the candy into 1-inch balls and store in an airtight container.

DEVILISH DIVINITY

Yield: 40

Heat Scale: Medium

This candy is light as air, but don't be fooled; it packs a powerful punch! This recipe is a tribute to Melissa's Grandma Pearl who worked magic in the kitchen when she made cakes, pies, and heavenly divinity.

$2^1/_2$ cups granulated sugar

$^1/_2$ cup water

$^1/_2$ cup light corn syrup

2 large egg whites

Pinch of cream of tartar

$^1/_4$ teaspoon habanero powder

1 cup finely chopped pine nuts

$1^1/_2$ teaspoons vanilla extract

In a medium heavy saucepan, heat the sugar, water, and corn syrup until the sugar is dissolved, stirring constantly with a wooden spoon. When the ingredients have dissolved, turn up the heat to medium-high, then place a candy thermometer in the mixture and cook without stirring until the temperature of the candy reaches 265°. This should take about 10 minutes.

While the mixture is cooking, place the egg whites in a mixing bowl and whip them with an electric mixer until they are frothy. Add the cream of tartar and habanero powder, and increase the speed of the mixer, beating until firm peaks form.

When the sugar mixture reaches 265°, remove it from the heat. Slowly pour the sugar mixture into the egg whites while continuing to mix on a slow speed. Be sure to pour the sugar mixture into the center of the bowl. When all of the sugar mixture is in the bowl, increase the speed of the mixer, and beat until the candy is firm, about 12 minutes. Stir in the pine nuts and the vanilla extract.

Line 2 baking sheets with waxed paper. Drop 2-inch wide spoonfuls of the candy onto the paper, leaving ample space between them. Let the candy set up at room temperature until firm, then store in an airtight container between sheets of waxed paper.

DOUBLE-TROUBLE CHOCOLATE TRUFFLES

Yield: About 4 dozen
Heat Scale: Medium

Fresh New Mexican green chile is the heat source in this tremendous treat. With the combination of baking chocolate and white chocolate, it's exceptionally wonderful to eat. Try substituting 2 teaspoons of cayenne powder to heat the truffles up even more.

8 ounces baking chocolate

4 ounces white chocolate chips

2 tablespoons granulated sugar

$^1/_4$ cup roasted, stemmed, seeded, and minced New Mexican green chile

$^1/_2$ teaspoon ground cinnamon

1 (14-ounce) can light sweetened condensed milk

Finely chopped pine nuts

Place both chocolates in a double boiler and melt them over the hot water, stirring until smooth. Add the sugar, green chile, cinnamon, and milk, mixing until very smooth. Remove the mixture from the heat and let it cool slightly.

Shape the chocolate mixture into 1-inch balls, then roll in the pine nuts. Chill the candy in the refrigerator in an airtight tin.

CASCABEL CARAMEL TURTLES

Yield: 24

Heat Scale: Medium

The word cascabel *means rattle in Spanish. This full-flavored dried chile probably received its name because of its shape and the way its seeds rattle when you shake it. These turtles are like no others you've tasted before; they offer a bit of sweet and a bit of heat to round out this most beloved candy.*

24 soft caramels

2 tablespoons frozen whipped topping

Butter-flavored vegetable cooking spray

72 pecan halves

4 ounces semisweet chocolate chips

6 cascabel chiles, stemmed, seeded, and finely ground

In a microwave-safe mixing bowl, combine the caramels and whipped topping, and cook on 50-percent power for 45 seconds. Remove and stir. Continue this process in 10-second increments until the mixture has melted and is smooth and well blended. Let it cool slightly.

Spray a baking sheet lightly with the cooking spray. Place the pecan halves on the sheet in groups of three, arranged so that each pecan group forms a "Y" shape, forming the turtle's head and legs. Carefully spoon the caramel mixture over each "Y" group, leaving the ends of the pecans showing. Set aside until the caramel is hard.

Place the chocolate chips in a microwave-safe bowl and microwave on 50-percent power for 45 seconds. Remove and stir, and repeat the process in 10-second intervals until the chocolate is melted and smooth. Stir in the cascabel powder, then let the chocolate mixture cool slightly. Spoon the melted chocolate over the caramel, being careful not to cover the exposed ends of the pecans. Set aside until hard, then store in a covered container in a cool place.

Note: When working with the melted caramels, we found it easier to coat our fingers with butter, roll the caramel into little balls, flatten them into "shells," and stick the pecans on the shells. This is a little extra work, but is a much easier way to handle the sticky caramel.

CASHEW CHILE BRITTLE

Yield: 4 cups
Heat Scale: Medium

This crunchy treat puts a new bite into a traditional candy. We love to make this and send it to relatives in far-away places. This candy keeps for up to 2 weeks in an airtight container, although we doubt you'll be able to keep your friends and family from eating it all within a day or two.

2 tablespoons safflower oil

2 cups granulated sugar

$^1/_2$ cup water

$^1/_2$ teaspoon cream of tartar

$^1/_2$ teaspoon New Mexican green chile powder

1 tablespoon New Mexican red chile powder

2 cups cashew nut halves, toasted

Using a baking sheet with sides or jelly roll pan, coat the sheet with the safflower oil, and set aside. In a medium saucepan, combine the sugar, water and cream of tartar. Cook the mixture over high heat, stirring continuously, until it turns a light golden color. Brush down the sides of the pan twice with a pastry brush dipped in water to prevent the mixture from crystallizing.

While stirring the mixture with a wooden spoon, add the chile powders and cashews. When the cashews are completely coated, remove the caramel from the heat and pour onto the oiled baking sheet, spreading it out with the wooden spoon. Do this step as quickly as possible, as the candy sets fast. Relax for the next 30 minutes while the brittle cools. Break the brittle into pieces with your hands. Store the candy in airtight containers.

HOT CHOCOLATE
FRUIT FONDUE

Yield: About 2 cups
Heat Scale: Hot

Fondue was very hip in the 1960s, and we're happy to report, in this age of retro everything, that fondue is making a comeback. If you're not quite ready to fork out the cash for a new fondue set, scout out a few garage sales—we almost guarantee you'll find a fondue pot or two.

9 ounces white chocolate

$^1/_4$ teaspoon habanero powder

$^1/_2$ cup whipping cream

2 tablespoons Grand Marnier

Assorted fruits of your choice (such as fresh pineapple, banana, papaya, mango, orange, kiwifruit), cut in bite-sized pieces

Place chocolate in a microwave-safe dish and microwave on 50-percent power for 1 minute. Remove and stir, continuing the process in 10-second increments until the chocolate is melted and smooth. When the chocolate is melted, stir in the habanero powder, cream, and Grand Marnier. Place the mixture in the fondue set, or in a chafing dish to keep warm. Dip your favorite fruits in the chocolate and enjoy!

CHILE-CHOCOLATE PRETZELS

Yield: 36
Heat Scale: Medium

Plain pretzels are one of Melissa's favorite foods in the world, so she was a little nervous to try them with chocolate on top, thus destroying the virtues of one of the best lowfat snacks around. Little did she know how wonderful these would turn out. Give them a try; if you like pretzels, you'll love this candy!

2 cups milk chocolate chips

1 teaspoon cayenne

2 tablespoons vegetable shortening

36 pretzels

In a microwave-safe bowl, combine the chocolate, cayenne powder, and vegetable shortening. Microwave on 50-percent power for 1 minute, then remove and stir. Continue this process in 10-second increments until the mixture is smooth and well blended. Dip the pretzels in the chocolate 1 at a time making certain to coat both sides. Place coated pretzels on waxed paper and chill in the refrigerator until hard.

RED CHILE
CARAMEL CORN

Yield: 8 to 10 cups
Heat Scale: Medium

This recipe was contributed by Nancy Gerlach, the food editor of Chile Pepper *magazine. You may adjust the heat of this dish by the type of chile used; New Mexican chiles will provide a mild heat while cayennes or chiles de arbol will produce a more fiery candy.*

> 3 cups granulated sugar
> $^1/_2$ cup light corn syrup
> 1 tablespoon New Mexican red chile powder
> $^1/_2$ cup popping corn
> Vegetable oil (for popping corn)
> 1 cup roasted peanuts, chopped
> 1 cup toasted almonds, chopped

Place sugar in a saucepan and add the corn syrup. Mix in the red chile and cook over medium heat until the sugar melts and is golden brown, about 30 to 45 minutes. Stir constantly, being careful to prevent mixture from burning.

Pop the corn in the vegetable oil. Toss the nuts with the popcorn.

Grease 2 large baking sheets with oil and spread the popcorn mixture on them. Slowly pour the sugar syrup evenly over the popcorn. Allow to cool and then break into pieces. Store in airtight tins.

AND IT'LL MAKE YOUR REFRIGERATOR SMELL BETTER TOO!

Peanut brittle was created in 1890 when a woman in New England accidentally added baking soda to her peanut taffy instead of cream of tartar. What she thought to be a disaster turned out to be the invention of peanut brittle.

NOT-SO-ENGLISH TOFFEE

Yield: About 36

Heat Scale: Hot

Preparing this candy is a snap. We think this delectable delight would most definitely shock the Queen. The best part of this treat is the slow afterburn from the candy that gets stuck in your back teeth.

$^3/_4$ cup finely chopped pecans or walnuts

1 cup unsalted butter

1 cup sugar

1 teaspoon habanero powder

2 tablespoons water

1 tablespoon light corn syrup

$^1/_4$ pound semisweet chocolate, coarsely chopped

Butter a 9 by 13-inch pan. Sprinkle half of the nuts over the bottom of the pan.

In a medium-sized, heavy saucepan insert a candy thermometer, add the butter, and melt over low heat. Whisk in the sugar; cook over low heat, stirring constantly until the mixture comes to a rolling boil. Stir in the habanero powder, water, and corn syrup, mixing well. Continue cooking, stirring often, until the mixture reaches 290°.

Pour candy into the prepared pan, spreading it evenly with the back of a spoon. While the toffee is cooling, place the chocolate pieces in a small mixing bowl, and microwave on 50-percent power for 25 seconds, then remove and stir with a plastic spatula. Continue to microwave in 10-second increments until the chocolate is melted. Be careful not to burn the chocolate. Spread the chocolate over the top of the toffee, and sprinkle on the remaining nuts. Refrigerate the candy until it sets. When the toffee is hard, cut it into squares, and store it in a covered container.

CHOCOLATE-TOPPED
ANCHO-ALMOND BRITTLE

Yield: 8 dozen

Heat Scale: Medium

Almond Roca, which inspired this brittle, was introduced by Haley and Brown of Tacoma, Washington, in 1923. However, they ran into trouble when they discovered the candy was susceptible to turning rancid, due to its high butter content. By 1928, Almond Roca was packaged in hermetically sealed tins, and the problem was solved.

1 cup butter

$3/4$ cup coarsely chopped blanched almonds

$1^1/4$ cups granulated sugar

2 teaspoons ancho powder

6 ounces milk chocolate chips

Melt the butter in a large saucepan over low heat; add the almonds and sugar. Increase the heat to high and continue to cook, stirring rapidly, until the sugar melts and the mixture becomes light tan in color. Stir in the ancho powder and remove the pan from the heat. Place a 9 by 13-inch baking pan in a 350° oven for 10 minutes. Remove the heated pan, pour the candy mixture into it, and spread evenly to a thickness of about $3/8$ inch.

Sprinkle the chocolate chips over the hot mixture and spread them evenly with a plastic spatula after they melt, then let the candy cool. Remove the candy by turning the pan upside down and hitting the bottom with a spoon. Break the candy into small pieces with a heavy spoon and store in an airtight container.

ISLAND SUGAR PLUMS

Yield: 24
Heat Scale: Medium

Since this recipe contains ginger, and since most of the ginger in the world comes from Jamaica, we have named these candies Island Sugar Plums. We have added pasilla chiles to this fantastic treat as it complements both the citrus and the raisiny overtones of this complex candy. These are perfect for a late-night snack on a holiday night.

4 cups coarsely chopped pitted dates

1 cup coarsely chopped raisins

1 cup coarsely chopped pecans

1 cup coarsely chopped pistachios

$^{1}/_{8}$ teaspoon ground ginger

$^{1}/_{3}$ cup stemmed, seeded, rehydrated, and minced pasilla chiles

$1^{1}/_{2}$ teaspoons grated orange zest

Brandy

Confectioners' sugar

Combine dates, raisins, pecans, pistachios, ginger, pasillas, and orange zest in a large mixing bowl. Add just enough brandy for the mixture to stick together. Shape the candy into 1-inch balls and roll each one in the confectioners' sugar. Store in an airtight container.

HEALTHY JALAPEÑO
CITRUS BITES

Yield: About 40

Heat Scale: Medium

Since we pledged to include at least one lowfat selection in each chapter, we have come up with this fresh and fruity confection for when you need a tasty change from chocolate. Chopped figs may be substituted for the dates if you wish.

1 cup lowfat granola

2 teaspoons jalapeño powder

$^1/_2$ cup chopped dates

$^1/_4$ cup finely chopped dried mangos

$^1/_4$ cup finely chopped dried pears

$^1/_4$ cup dried apricots

$^1/_2$ cup coarsely chopped pecans

$^1/_4$ cup coarsely chopped pistachio nuts

2 tablespoons orange juice

1 teaspoon lemon juice

$^1/_2$ teaspoon grated orange zest

Flaked unsweetened coconut

In a large mixing bowl, mix together the granola, jalapeño powder, fruits, nuts, orange juice, lemon juice, and orange zest. Moisten your hands with a bit of water and form 1-inch balls from the mixture. Roll in the coconut and store on waxed paper in an airtight container.

HOT CANDIED ORANGE PEEL

Yield: About $1^1/_2$ cups
Heat Scale: Medium   🔥 🔥

Use the leftover peel from making orange-based recipes to create this spicy delight. Serve the peel as a garnish or accompaniment to any cake, pie, or ice cream in this book.

2 cups orange peel

1 cup granulated sugar

$^1/_4$ cup light corn syrup

$^1/_2$ cup water

$^1/_2$ teaspoon habanero powder

$^1/_4$ teaspoon ground ginger

With a small paring knife, strip the white membrane from orange peel and discard. Cut the cleaned peel into strips 1 inch wide and set aside.

Combine the sugar, corn syrup, water, chile, and ginger in a small saucepan. Bring the mixture to a boil and cook until it reaches 290° on a candy thermometer. Drop the strips of peel into the syrup and cook for 10 minutes (or until skin is slightly transparent). While peel is cooking, grease two baking sheets. Drop the pieces of peel on the baking sheets and allow to cool and dry. Store covered in a glass jar at room temperature.

QUICK FIERCE FUDGE

Yield: 4 dozen
Heat Scale: Medium

There's no need for a messy double boiler with this easy recipe. Melissa always makes lots of this decadent dessert over the holidays. It's wonderful because one bite is so rich that you might be able to stop after just one piece.

3 cups semisweet chocolate morsels

1 (14-ounce) can sweetened condensed milk

3 teaspoons New Mexican red chile powder, Chimayó preferred

$^1/_4$ cup butter, cut into pieces

1 cup chopped walnuts

Combine chocolate morsels, condensed milk, red chile powder, and butter in a 2-quart glass bowl. Microwave on 50-percent power for 4 to 5 minutes, stirring at $1^1/_2$ minute intervals. Once the chocolate is completely melted, remove from the microwave and stir in the walnuts, and pour into a buttered 8-inch square dish. Chill for at least 2 hours. Cut into squares and store in an airtight container.

FOLLOW YOUR NOSE TO THE CHOCOLATE

Thinking of putting that left-over fudge in the refrigerator next to the garlic? Think again. Candy is known to pick up the odors of whatever is in close proximity to it. So unless it is stored properly in an airtight container, you may be highly disappointed on your return trip to the fudge. Chocolate should be stored at room temperature, wrapped in foil or brown paper or inside an airtight tin.

ISLAND SQUARES

Yield: About 16

Heat Scale: Hot   🔥 🔥 🔥

This candy combines two of the best products from Hawaii: coconut and macadamia nuts. Then the addition of Scotch bonnets gives each piece an extra zip. Remember to be very careful when mincing these ferocious chiles. You may want to mince them in a food processor to chop them in the easiest and safest manner possible.

- 1 cup semisweet chocolate chips
- 2 tablespoons shortening
- 1 Scotch bonnet or habanero chile, stemmed, seeded, and finely minced
- 1 (14-ounce) can light sweetened condensed milk
- .25 ounce unflavored gelatin
- 6 cups flaked unsweetened coconut
- $^1/_2$ cup chopped macadamia nuts

Grease an 8-inch square glass pan with butter, making sure to coat the sides and the bottom.

Combine the chocolate chips, shortening, and habanero in a microwave-safe mixing bowl and cook on 50-percent power for 30 seconds. Remove and stir. Continue this process, cooking in 10-second increments until the mixture is melted, smooth, and well blended. Quickly spread half of the chocolate mixture in the pan. Chill in the refrigerator until it is hard; set the other half of the chocolate mixture aside.

In a heavy saucepan, combine the milk and gelatin, and heat to boiling, stirring constantly to dissolve the gelatin. When the gelatin is completely dissolved, remove mixture from heat and stir in the coconut and the macadamia nuts. Let the mixture cool to a slightly warm temperature.

Remove the chocolate from the refrigerator. Spread the milk mixture over the chocolate in the pan, to cover, then spread the remaining half of the chocolate mixture over the milk mixture. Set aside to cool. Cut the candy into 2-inch squares, then wrap each candy individually in colored foil.

2

COOKIES CALIENTE

Cookies were transformed from dried-out biscuits to their current fabulous form many years ago. According to the *Food Lover's Companion*, the word cookie comes from the Dutch *koekje*, meaning "little cake." One of the essential components of most cookie recipes is sugar. So it makes sense that Persia, which was one of the first countries to cultivate sugar, was also one of the first countries to create a cookie-style cake.

Cookies are a mainstay of many households around the world. They are a comfort food that kids of all ages are absolutely crazy about. Chewy or chocolatey, in a bar, ball, or cut out, the smell of cookies baking is a tantalizing invitation to warmth, kindred spirit, and home.

And what would a cookie be without a glass of milk? Our fiery cookies are the perfect combination for this cool-down of custom. A regular cookie is sure to warm your heart; our spiced-up versions are guaranteed to warm the soul!

"I am still convinced that a good, simple, home-made cookie is preferable to all the store-bought cookies one can find."

—James Beard

RED CHILE
CASHEW CRUNCHIES

Yield: 7 dozen

Heat Scale: Medium

Cayenne is the ingredient that brings on the heat in these crunchy cookies. Put a little Arizona Chiltepin Ice Cream (page 181) between two cookies for a hot ice cream sandwich.

1 cup butter, softened

$^3/_4$ cup firmly packed light brown sugar

$^1/_2$ cup granulated sugar

2 tablespoons New Mexican red chile powder

1 egg

1 teaspoon vanilla extract

$2^1/_4$ cups all-purpose flour

$^1/_2$ teaspoon baking soda

$^1/_2$ teaspoon cream of tartar

$1^1/_2$ cups finely chopped cashews

Preheat oven to 350°.

In a large mixing bowl, beat the butter at medium speed with an electric mixer. Gradually add sugars, mixing well. Next add the chile powder, egg, and vanilla, then beat well. In a separate bowl, combine the flour, soda, and cream of tartar; gradually add to creamed mixture, mixing after each addition. Stir in the cashews.

Drop dough by rounded teaspoonfuls onto lightly greased baking sheets. Bake for 10 to 12 minutes or until lightly browned. Cool on wire racks.

HABANERO
MANGO-WALNUT COOKIES

Yield: 6 dozen

Heat Scale: Hot

Another highly heated treat, these cookies are especially good since they combine our favorite fruit, the mango, with the equally fruity but fiercely hot heat of the habanero. Substitute pine nuts for the walnuts for a nice change of pace.

4 cups all-purpose flour

2 cups sifted confectioners' sugar

1 cup cornstarch

2 cups butter

2 cups walnuts, chopped

2 egg yolks

$^1/_2$ teaspoon minced fresh habanero chile

1 tablespoon grated orange zest

5 tablespoons mango juice

Granulated sugar

Commercial cream cheese vanilla frosting

Preheat oven to 350°.

In a large mixing bowl stir together the flour, confectioners' sugar, and cornstarch. Using a pastry blender or two blunt edged knives, cut in the butter until the mixture resembles coarse crumbs. Next, stir in the nuts. In a separate bowl, combine the egg yolks, habanero, orange zest, and 4 tablespoons of the mango juice. Add the flour mixture, stirring until moistened. If necessary, add the remaining juice to moisten.

On a lightly floured surface, knead the dough until it forms a ball. Shape the dough into $1^1/_4$-inch balls, and arrange on ungreased baking sheets. Flatten balls by pressing with the bottom of a glass to $^1/_4$ inch thickness, dipping the glass into granulated sugar for each round.

Bake for 12 to 15 minutes or until the edges begin to brown. Transfer the cookies from baking sheets and cool on wire racks. Frost with the cream cheese vanilla frosting. If desired, garnish with finely grated orange zest.

SEARING SCOTTISH SHORTBREAD

Yield: 8

Heat Scale: Hot

This shortbread is long on heat, as it sports enough habaneros to surprise a taste bud or two. The ingredients are deceptively simple; who would know that these are some of the richest tasting cookies in the world?

$^1/_4$ cup melted butter

1 cup butter, room temperature

$^1/_2$ teaspoon habanero powder

$^1/_4$ cup confectioners' sugar

$^1/_4$ cup granulated sugar

1 teaspoon vanilla extract

$^1/_3$ cup rice flour

$1^2/_3$ cups all-purpose flour

Preheat oven to 325°. Brush a 10-inch stoneware shortbread mold or an 8- or 9-inch springform pan with the melted butter.

In a large bowl, beat together the butter, habanero powder, confectioners' sugar, granulated sugar, and vanilla until the mixture is light and fluffy. Add the rice flour and all-purpose flour to the mixture. Using your hands, work dough together until it is smooth and no longer crumbly; be careful not to overwork it. Pat the dough evenly into the buttered mold or pan.

Bake for 35 to 45 minutes or until light golden and still somewhat springy to the touch. Cool 15 minutes in mold, then gently loosen the shortbread. If using a springform pan, do not invert; cool in the pan on a rack. While slightly warm, cut shortbread into 8 wedges.

SERIOUS SHORTBREAD WITH
FRESH FRUIT-HABANERO TOPPING

Yield: 12 pieces

Heat Scale: Hot

🔥 🔥 🔥

Have you ever met a kiwifruit or mango that you haven't liked? We hope not, because they make up the bulk of the fantastic fruit topping that we've paired with our simple shortbread.

$^3/_4$ cup butter

$^1/_3$ cup confectioners' sugar

$1^1/_2$ cups flour

Fresh Fruit-Habanero Topping (page 139)

Preheat the oven to 350°.

In a large bowl, blend the butter, flour, and sugar to make a soft dough. Pat into a 10-inch quiche pan, and prick all over. Bake for 15 to 20 minutes. Remove from the oven and cool on a wire rack. Cut the shortbread and top each piece with some of the fruit topping.

CHILE POWDERS

All chiles can be dried and ground into powder; and in fact, most are, including the habanero. To grind your own powders from dried chiles, simply put them in a coffee grinder or spice grinder. You may want to wear a painter's mask to protect your nose and mouth from the powder. After you have removed all of the powder from the electric grinder, mill white rice in the grinder and wipe it out. The rice will remove all chile remnants.

Powders are wonderful to have around because they are concentrated and take up very little space. We like to store then in small, airtight bottles. However, be sure not to grind up too many chiles because the fresher the powders the better the taste.

GREEN-CHILE CHOCOLATE-CHUNK PECAN COOKIES

Yield: 36

Heat Scale: Hot ♨ ♨ ♨

Move over, Mrs. Fields. There's a new chocolate chunk cookie in town, and it's hot! Actually, this is one of Melissa's favorite cookies. She almost always takes them to a party when she is asked to bring something for dessert.

$^{1}/_{2}$ pound unsalted butter, softened

1 cup firmly packed light brown sugar

$^{3}/_{4}$ cup of granulated sugar

2 eggs, beaten

1 tablespoon vanilla extract

$2^{1}/_{2}$ cups all-purpose flour

$^{1}/_{2}$ teaspoon salt

$^{1}/_{2}$ teaspoon baking powder

$^{1}/_{2}$ teaspoon baking soda

4 tablespoons green chile powder

3 cups semisweet chocolate chunks

1 cup chopped pecans

Preheat oven to 375°.

In a large mixing bowl, combine the butter, sugars, eggs, and vanilla, and cream with an electric mixer. In a separate bowl, sift together the flour, salt, baking powder, baking soda, and green chile powder. When combined, gradually add the flour mixture to batter, and beat until just combined and smooth. Next, add the chocolate chunks and nuts. Drop the batter in tablespoonsful onto greased baking sheets and bake until light golden brown, or about 10 minutes. Remove from baking sheets while hot, and cool on wire racks. Serve warm or cooled with milk—lots of milk.

COCONUT-HAZELNUT-
SERRANO BISCOTTI

Yield: 36

Heat Scale: Medium

These twice-baked delicacies are wonderful when served with any of the popular coffee drinks, or one of our specialties from Chapter 9. Feel free to substitute 2 teaspoons of New Mexican red chile powder for the jalapeño.

$^1/_2$ cup unsalted butter, softened

$^3/_4$ cup firmly packed brown sugar

2 large eggs

1 serrano chile, stemmed, seeded, and minced

$^1/_2$ cup sweetened shredded coconut

$2^1/_4$ cups all-purpose flour

$1^1/_2$ teaspoons baking powder

$^1/_4$ teaspoon salt

1 cup chopped hazelnuts (about 4 ounces)

In a large mixing bowl, cream the butter and sugar with an electric mixture. Add the eggs 1 at a time, beating well after each addition. Beat in the serrano and coconut. In a separate bowl, combine the flour, baking powder, and salt. Gradually stir these ingredients into the butter mixture. Next, mix in the hazelnuts. Cover and refrigerate the dough for 30 minutes.

Preheat oven to 350°. Line a baking sheet with parchment paper, and set aside.

Turn the dough out onto a floured work surface, then divide it in half. Shape each half into a 2-inch wide log. Transfer the logs onto the prepared baking sheet, spacing evenly. Bake for about 35 minutes, until the logs are golden brown, and firm to the touch. Cool the logs about 20 minutes on the sheet.

Reduce oven temperature to 325°. Transfer the logs to a work surface. Discard the parchment. Cut each log diagonally into $^1/_2$-inch-thick slices. Arrange the cookies flat sides down on unlined baking sheets. Bake until crisp and golden brown, about 15 minutes. Transfer cookies to racks and cool completely.

Note: For a variation, substitute chopped almonds for the hazelnuts. Also, experiment by dipping the biscotti in different types of melted chocolate.

LEMON FIRE CRISPS

Yield: 6 dozen
Heat Scale: Medium

Another culinary creation of our friend Nancy Gerlach, who says she often surprises people with these hot citrus cookies. The heat of the chile is not evident at first; it builds as you eat more cookies.

1 cup butter, softened

$^1/_2$ cup granulated sugar

1 tablespoon lemon juice

1 tablespoon grated lemon zest

1 egg

$2^1/_4$ cups all-purpose flour

$^1/_2$ teaspoon cayenne powder

$^1/_4$ teaspoon salt

$^1/_4$ teaspoon baking soda

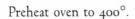

Preheat oven to 400°.

Cream the butter and sugar until light and fluffy. Add the lemon juice, lemon zest, and egg, and beat well.

Sift together the flour, cayenne powder, salt, and baking soda. Beat into the butter mixture.

Place the mixture into a cookie press, and force the dough onto ungreased baking sheets. Bake for 8 minutes or until the cookies are lightly browned.

CHOCOLATE-DIPPED PINE NUT GOOD LUCK COOKIES

🌶 🌶 🌶

These cookies are certainly a mighty interesting twist on a fancy cookie favorite. The horseshoe shape makes them lucky; feel free to vary the type of chile powder to change the heat level and taste. Note: This recipe is a little more difficult than the others and requires the use of a pastry bag.

6 ounces pine nuts, lightly crushed

7 ounces almond paste, cut in 1-inch pieces

1 cup granulated sugar

2 large egg whites

10 ounces bittersweet or semisweet chocolate chips, chopped

2 teaspoons cayenne powder

Preheat oven to 375°. On a large baking sheet, spread out $^1/_{14}$ of the pine nuts in a long line.

Combine the almond paste and sugar in a food processor and process until blended. Gradually blend in the egg whites.

Spoon the dough into a pastry bag fitted with a medium (no. 6) plain round tip. Pipe one 6-inch long segment of dough on top of the pine nuts on the baking sheet. Gently roll the dough in the pine nuts, coating completely. Transfer the dough segment to a large, clean baking sheet, bending the ends to create a horseshoe shape. Repeat with remaining dough and pine nuts, spacing cookies 1 inch apart. Bake until golden brown, about 15 minutes. Transfer to rack and cool completely.

Line a large baking sheet with foil. Place the chocolate in a microwave-safe bowl and microwave on 50-percent power for 1 minute. Remove and stir, repeating the process in 20-second increments until the chocolate is melted and smooth. When all of the chocolate is melted, stir in the cayenne powder. Dip the ends of 1 cookie into the chocolate, then shake the cookie gently to remove any excess chocolate. Place the cookie flat side down on the prepared baking sheet. Repeat with remaining cookies. Refrigerate until the chocolate sets.

NUCLEAR MACAROONS

Yield: 24

Heat Scale: Extremely hot

The habanero raises the heat level of these cookies and makes them catch fire in the back of the throat. But don't worry, they're not too hot to enjoy, especially when followed with a milk chaser.

3 cups sweetened flaked coconut

1 cup macadamia nuts, chopped

1 cup light sweetened condensed milk

1 teaspoon vanilla extract

1 teaspoon habanero powder

2 egg whites

Pinch of salt

Preheat oven to 350°. Place coconut and macadamia nuts on a large baking sheet. Bake until lightly toasted, stirring frequently, about 10 minutes; remove from the oven and set aside.

Grease 2 large baking sheets. In a separate large mixing bowl, combine the condensed milk, vanilla and habanero powder. Add the coconut and macadamia nuts to the mixture and combine well. Using an electric mixer, beat the egg whites and salt until stiff but not dry; carefully fold into the coconut mixture.

Drop batter by rounded tablespoonfuls onto prepared baking sheets. Bake for about 13 minutes, until the cookies are just barely golden brown. Cool completely on the baking sheet.

ISLAND SPICE COOKIES

Yield: 36

Heat Scale: Medium

♨ ♨

These cookies combine Caribbean islanders' love of sweets with the East Indian spice influence on the West Indies.

1 cup unsalted butter, softened

$^2/_3$ cup firmly packed light brown sugar

$1^1/_2$ teaspoons finely ground black pepper

$1^1/_2$ teaspoons ground coriander

$^1/_2$ teaspoon anise seeds, finely chopped

$^1/_2$ teaspoon ground ginger

$^1/_2$ teaspoon ground cinnamon

$^1/_2$ teaspoon ground allspice

1 teaspoon cayenne powder, or $^1/_2$ teaspoon habanero powder

$^1/_2$ teaspoon salt

1 teaspoon vanilla extract

2 teaspoons finely grated lime zest

2 cups all-purpose flour

Preheat oven to 350°.

In a large bowl, cream the butter and brown sugar. Stir in the black pepper, coriander, anise, ginger, cinnamon, allspice, cayenne, salt, vanilla, and lime zest. Next, add the flour and mix well. Cover the dough in plastic wrap and place in the freezer for about 10 minutes.

Remove the dough from the freezer, unwrap, scoop it out into balls, and place them on baking sheets, flattening them slightly with the back of the spoon. Set aside for 10 minutes.

Bake the cookies for about 18 minutes, until they are golden brown on the bottom and firm but not hard to the touch. Let the cookies cool on the baking sheets for about 1 minute before transferring to a wire rack to cool completely.

SNAPPY GINGER
SUGAR COOKIES

Yield: 4 dozen

Heat Scale: Medium ♨ ♨

Who says sugar cookies are old-fashioned and boring? We've peppered up an old recipe with lots of ginger and a chile or two. Note: This recipe requires advance preparation as the dough is easier to handle if you make it the day before and refrigerate it before rolling, cutting, and baking.

$^1/_2$ cup butter or margarine

1 cup granulated sugar

1 egg

2 tablespoons milk

$^1/_2$ teaspoon vanilla extract

2 teaspoons ground ginger

2 teaspoons jalapeño powder

$^1/_2$ teaspoon salt

2 teaspoons baking powder

$1^3/_4$ cups all-purpose flour

3 tablespoons minced crystallized ginger

Preheat oven to 375°. Grease 2 baking sheets and set aside.

Let the butter stand at room temperature to soften. In a medium mixing bowl, cream the butter and sugar until light and fluffy. Beat egg, milk, and vanilla into the butter mixture. Sift together the ginger, jalapeño powder, salt, baking powder, and flour and add to the butter mixture, a little at a time, until well blended. Beat in the crystallized ginger.

Wrap the dough in plastic wrap and refrigerate until firm and chilled, preferably overnight. Roll out the dough to $^1/_4$-inch thick and cut with a cookie cutter. Bake on prepared baking sheets for about 8 minutes.

3

▲▲▲▲▲▲▲▲▲▲▲▲▲▲▲▲▲▲▲▲▲▲▲▲▲▲▲▲▲▲▲▲▲▲▲▲▲▲▲

POTENT PUDDINGS
& CUSTARDS

Puddings have a long culinary history and probably originated from early gruels or porridges. Nowadays, pudding is a general term for soft, sweetened foods, so in actuality all the desserts in this chapter are puddings. A custard is a puddinglike dessert usually made with sweetened milk and eggs that can either be baked in a hot water bath or cooked on top of the stove in a double boiler.

Mousse is the French word for "froth" or "foam," and generally means a light and fluffy dessert made with beaten egg whites and whipped cream. Mousses are usually cold, but there are hot mousses, which are baked in a hot water bath. *Flan* is the Spanish and Mexican baked custard that is coated with caramel, and a *brûlée* is simply a broiled or "burned" custard.

Now that we're done with definitions, let's proceed to the rewards. First, we offer the informal mousses then some flans, which were a lot of fun. Next, you'll find our brûlée, which burns in more ways than one.

People sometimes think that all bread puddings are the same, but we beg to differ. Chiles and a few other ingredients can create some delicious variations. We conclude our plethora of puddings with those made with rice—savory treats you're sure to love.

ANCHO CHOCOLATE MOUSSE
WITH GRAND MARNIER

Yield: 6 servings
Heat Scale: Mild

Ah, there's nothing like a mousse to complete a dinner, and this one is spiked with the raisiny flavors of ancho chile. You can use other chiles, but only pasilla powder has flavor similar to ancho.

4 ounces sweet baking chocolate

4 ounces semisweet chocolate

$^1/_4$ cup Grand Marnier or other orange-flavored liqueur

1 teaspoon freshly ground ancho chile powder

2 cups whipping cream

$^1/_2$ cup sifted confectioners' sugar

Semisweet chocolate curls for garnish

Combine the chocolates, Grand Marnier, and ancho powder in a heavy saucepan and cook over low heat until chocolate melts, stirring constantly. Remove from the heat and cool to lukewarm.

Beat the whipping cream, adding the confectioners' sugar, until soft peaks form. Gently fold about $^1/_4$ of the whipped cream into the chocolate, then fold in the remaining whipped cream. Spoon the mousse into individual serving dishes and chill until ready to serve. Garnish with semisweet chocolate curls.

POWERFUL PEAR
AND CHOCOLATE MOUSSE

Yield: 6 to 8 servings

Heat Scale: Hot

Further exploring the range of chocolate in mousses, we combine it with pears and habaneros in this dessert.

2 large fresh California Bartlett pears, pared, cored, and chopped

$^1/_2$ habanero chile, stemmed and seeded

1 envelope unflavored gelatin

6 tablespoons granulated sugar

$^1/_4$ teaspoon salt

3 large eggs, separated

1 ounce semisweet chocolate, cut in pieces

1 teaspoon vanilla extract

$^1/_2$ teaspoon unsweetened chocolate extract

$^1/_8$ teaspoon ground cinnamon

$^1/_2$ cup whipping cream

Whipped cream and chocolate curls for garnish

In a food processor or blender, purée the pears and the habanero chile, then measure out $1^1/_4$ cups. In a double boiler, combine the gelatin, 2 tablespoons of the sugar, and the salt. Beat the egg yolks lightly and add to the gelatin mixture, along with the puréed pears. Mix well.

Cook in a double boiler, stirring constantly, about 5 minutes, until slightly thickened. Add the chocolate pieces and stir until the chocolate melts. Remove from the heat and stir in the vanilla, chocolate extract, and cinnamon. Cool until mixture thickens slightly.

In a bowl, beat the egg whites with a mixer until they form soft peaks. Gradually beat in the remaining 4 tablespoons of sugar, forming to a soft meringue. In another bowl, beat the cream to soft peaks. Fold the meringue and cream into the thickened gelatin mixture. Turn into a

6-inch soufflé dish 3 inches deep, or into a greased 1-quart mold and chill until firm, at least 3 hours. Shortly before serving, garnish with the whipped cream and chocolate curls.

DARK CHOCOLATE AND RED CHILE MOUSSE WITH LEMON LIQUEUR

Yield: 4 servings
Heat Scale: Medium

Dare we mix the flavors of chocolate, lemon, and red chile? You bet! Here is a mousse that is extremely simple to make, yet has a very complex taste.

4 ounces dark sweet chocolate

2 ounces unsweetened baking chocolate

7 tablespoons lemon liqueur

1 teaspoon New Mexican red chile powder

5 eggs, separated

Lemon slices for garnish

Lightly butter a saucepan, place it over low heat, and add the 2 chocolates. As the chocolate starts to melt, add 5 tablespoons of the lemon liqueur and the chile powder. When the chocolate is completely melted, add the egg yolks, one at a time, mixing well after each addition. Remove from heat and add the remaining 2 tablespoons of lemon liqueur. Mix gently.

Beat the egg whites with an electric mixer until they form soft peaks and fold thoroughly into the chocolate mixture. Pour into a 2-quart soufflé dish and refrigerate for at least 2 hours. Serve garnished with the lemon slices.

APRICOT-HABANERO MOUSSE

Yield: 8 to 10 servings
Heat Scale: Medium

Many sources say that the habanero chile has apricot-flavored over-tones. Well, in this dessert it really does! Note: *This recipe requires advance preparation.*

20 ladyfingers

3 (16-ounce) cans apricot halves

2 envelopes unflavored gelatin

5 egg yolks

$1^1/_4$ cups granulated sugar

$^1/_8$ teaspoon salt

1 cup milk

2 tablespoons apricot brandy or light rum

1 (2-ounce) package slivered almonds

$^1/_2$ habanero chile, stemmed, seeded, and
   puréed with a little water

$1^1/_2$ cups whipping cream

$3/_4$ cup whipping cream

2 tablespoons confectioners' sugar

$^1/_8$ teaspoon almond extract

Reserved apricots for garnish

Whole mint leaves for garnish

Sliced toasted almonds for garnish

Cut a 30 by 3-inch strip of waxed paper and line the sides of a 9-inch springform pan with the strip. Split the ladyfingers in half lengthwise and line the sides and bottom of the pan with them.

Drain the apricots, reserving $^1/_2$ cup of juice. Set aside 4 apricot halves for garnish. Add the remaining apricots to a food processor and purée for 1 minute. Set aside. Sprinkle the gelatin over the reserved $^1/_2$ cup of apricot juice and set aside. Combine egg yolks, $3/4$ cup of the sugar, and salt in a saucepan. Gradually add the milk and cook over medium heat, stirring constantly, for about 4 minutes, or until mixture thickens. Add the softened gelatin, stirring until it dissolves. Stir in puréed apricots, brandy, slivered almonds, and puréed habanero and mix well. Chill mixture for about 30 minutes.

In a bowl, using a mixer, beat the $1^1/_2$ cups of whipping cream, gradually adding the remaining $1/_2$ cup sugar, until soft peaks form. Fold the whipped cream into apricot mixture and spoon into the springform pan. Chill, covered, for 8 hours in the refrigerator.

Remove the ring from the springform pan, remove the waxed paper, and slide the mousse onto a serving plate. In a bowl, beat the $3/4$ cup of whipping cream, gradually adding the confectioners' sugar and almond extract, until soft peaks form. Pipe or dollop the whipped cream on top of the mousse. Slice the reserved apricots and arrange on top of the whipped cream. Garnish with the fresh mint leaves and a few toasted almonds.

THE OLD HOT WATER BATH TRICK

"Custards and creams are usually baked in a hot water bath or bain-marie (so called because Queen Marie Antoinette allegedly bathed in the palace kitchen's hot water after the staff finished serving meals). The technique promotes slow, even heating of the custard and prevents a hard, thick crust from forming on top. It is important to start with hot water; since water is denser than air, hot water conducts heat more effectively than hot air. This way, the side of the custard will cook before the top, which is only in contact with hot air, can begin to brown or burn."

—*Roger Hayot*

PUNGENT PLUM
AND PEACH AMBROSIA

Yield: 6 to 8 servings
Heat Scale: Medium

Here's a fruit-dominated mousse if ever there was one. Also dominating is the soft burn of the chile powder that's blended into the whipped cream. This recipe is extremely simple to make.

2 cups whipping cream

$^1/_3$ cup confectioners' sugar

2 teaspoons vanilla extract

$^1/_2$ teaspoon habanero powder

2 cups pitted and diced ripe plums

2 bananas, peeled and sliced

1 cup peeled, pitted, and diced ripe peaches

$^1/_3$ cup pecan or walnut halves

2 navel oranges, peeled and sectioned

Plum and peach slices for garnish

In a large bowl, using an electric mixer, whip the cream with sugar, vanilla, and chile powder until stiff peaks form. Fold in the remaining ingredients. Spoon the mixture into a serving bowl and chill for at least 3 hours. Serve garnished with plum and peach slices.

CAFE DIABLE MOUSSE

Yield: 4 servings
Heat Scale: Mild

Here is a great way to turn a dessert drink into a dessert mousse. Then, of course, you could serve the Cafe Diable (page 157) with this mousse for a double whammy of a finish to a meal.

4 egg whites

1 pint whipping cream

$^1/_2$ cup granulated sugar

1 tablespoon unflavored gelatin

5 tablespoons Cafe Diable (page 157)

Freshly ground nutmeg for garnish

In a bowl, beat the egg whites with an electric mixer until very stiff. In another bowl, beat the cream just until peaks form. Slowly beat the sugar into the whipped cream then fold the mixture into the egg whites.

Dissolve the gelatin in the Cafe Diable and then gradually fold into the cream and egg white mixture. Spoon into 4 individual stemmed dessert dishes or wine glasses and chill for at least 2 hours before serving. Serve sprinkled with the nutmeg.

HAWAIIAN VINTAGE CHOCOLATE SPICY SOUFFLÉ

Yield: 4 servings
Heat Scale: Mild

Hawaiian Vintage Chocolate will make you want to forsake any other chocolate forever. Below is the recipe we collected from the Menele Bay Hotel in Lanai, Hawaii. Chef Philip Padovani created this recipe to showcase the only chocolate made from cacao beans grown in the United States. You can order Hawaiian Vintage Chocolate in 1-pound quantities by calling 800-735-8494.

- 6 tablespoons granulated sugar
- 3 ounces Hawaiian Vintage bittersweet chocolate or your favorite chocolate, melted
- 4 teaspoons cognac
- 4 egg yolks
- 8 egg whites
- Confectioners' sugar
- 2 teaspoons New Mexican red chile powder

Preheat oven to 375°. Grease the sides of four 4-inch ramekins and then coat each with 2 tablespoons of the sugar.

Combine the chocolate, cognac, and egg yolks in a bowl.

In a separate bowl, whip the egg whites with the remaining 4 tablespoons sugar until peaks form. Using a spatula, fold the egg whites into the chocolate mixture, and mix carefully.

Pour the mixture into the bowls and bake for 12 minutes or until the soufflés are firm.

In a small bowl, mix the confectioners' sugar and red chile. Sprinkle the soufflés with the confectioners' sugar and chile mixture and serve immediately.

Cascabel Caramel Turtles (top),
Devilish Divinity (center), and
Cashew Chile Brittle (bottom)

Green-Chile Chocolate-Chunk Pecan Cookies (left) and Coconut-Hazelnut-Serrano Biscotti (right)

HABANERO-
CREAM CHEESE FLAN

Yield: 8 servings

Heat Scale: Medium

This recipe shows how easy it is to spice up a custard—just add a little chile powder. Virtually any chile powder can be used as long as it's pure ground dried chile and not "chili" powder, which has cumin and other spices added.

1 cup granulated sugar

$^1/_2$ cup water

6 eggs

$1^3/_4$ cups water

1 (14-ounce) can sweetened condensed milk

1 (8-ounce) package cream cheese, at room temperature

$^1/_2$ teaspoon habanero powder

Ground cinnamon for garnish

Preheat oven to 300°.

Combine the sugar and water in small, heavy saucepan and cook over low heat, stirring occasionally, until the sugar dissolves. Increase the heat and boil until syrup is golden brown, about 8 minutes. Pour into 8 or 9-inch round ovenproof glass or porcelain baking dish, swirling to coat bottom of dish. Cool caramel completely.

Combine eggs, water, milk, cream cheese, and habanero powder in a blender and purée until smooth. Pour this mixture into caramel-lined dish, and place the dish in a water bath. Bake until a knife inserted in the center of the custard comes our clean, about 70 minutes. Cover and refrigerate until well chilled.

Gently press the edges of the custard with spoon to loosen from sides of dish. Invert custard onto platter. Serve chilled, garnished with cinnamon.

PINE NUT FLAN WITH RED CHILE CARAMEL SAUCE

Yield: 6 servings
Heat Scale: Mild

Flan is a traditional Mexican custard dessert that has been adopted by cooks throughout the Southwest.

2 cups granulated sugar

$^2/_3$ cup water

$3^1/_2$ cups whole milk

1 vanilla bean

6 eggs

1 teaspoon ground cinnamon

1 teaspoon ground nutmeg

1 teaspoon ground ginger

1 teaspoon New Mexican red chile powder

1 tablespoon dark rum

1 cup whole shelled pine nuts

Preheat the oven to 350°.

Place 1 cup of the sugar and the water in a heavy saucepan, and stir over low heat until the sugar is dissolved. Gradually increase the heat and boil until the mix is light brown. Reduce the heat and simmer until the syrup is an amber color, swirling the pan occasionally to push any crystals back in the syrup. Allow to cool slightly and pour evenly into 6 warmed custard cups so that this caramel sauce coats them.

Scald the milk and vanilla bean. Remove from heat and allow to cool. Remove the vanilla bean.

In a bowl, beat the eggs, cinnamon, nutmeg, ginger, chile powder, and rum together until foamy. Whisk in the remaining 1 cup of sugar and the pine nuts. Gradually add the milk, stirring until the sugar is dissolved.

Pour the mixture into the custard cups. Place the cups in a hot water bath. Bake for 60 to 70 minutes or until a thin knife inserted halfway between the center and the edge of the custard comes out clean.

Run a thin knife around the outside of the cup and invert the custard onto a dish. Let sit at room temperature for 10 minutes before serving.

COCONUT-GINGER FLAN WITH ANCHO

Yield: 6 servings

Heat Scale: Mild

This recipe is adapted from Susana Trilling, who owns the Seasons of My Heart Cooking School at Rancho Aurora in Oaxaca, Mexico. She prepares it a day ahead and serves it ice cold.

$^1/_4$ cup plus 3 tablespoons granulated sugar

$^1/_2$ cup sliced almonds

2 (12-ounce) cans coconut milk (not sweetened coconut syrup)

$^1/_2$ cup milk

6 eggs

5 egg yolks

$^1/_4$ teaspoon vanilla extract

1 teaspoon freshly ground ancho chile powder

1 tablespoon minced crystallized ginger

Preheat oven to 350°.

In a sauté pan over medium heat melt 3 tablespoons of the sugar until brown and bubbly; do not stir. Pour syrup into a round, 9-inch flan pan and rotate the pan so the syrup completely covers the bottom. Place the almonds on the syrup and set aside.

Combine the coconut milk, remaining sugar, milk, eggs, egg yolks, vanilla, and ancho powder; whisk well. Add the ginger, stir well, and pour the mixture into the pan. Place the pan in a hot water bath, cover with aluminum foil, and bake for 1 hour. Remove from the oven and chill. To serve, flip the pan over on a platter, slice thinly, and garnish with ginger.

ORANGE AND CHOCOLATE
FIERY FLAN

Yield: 6 to 8 servings

Heat Scale: Medium

Here's an unusual dessert, a baked crust containing a cooked but unbaked flan—or maybe it's more of a mousse. Note: This recipe requires advance preparation.

$^1/_2$ cup butter

$1^1/_2$ cups all-purpose flour

6 tablespoons superfine sugar

3 tablespoons water, approximately

Pinto beans (for baking crust)

$^1/_4$ cup plain all-purpose flour

3 tablespoons unsweetened cocoa

1 tablespoon vanilla extract

Grated zest and juice of 1 orange

3 egg yolks

2 teaspoons freshly ground ancho chile powder

$1^1/_4$ cups milk

4 ounces semisweet dark chocolate, melted

$1^1/_4$ cups whipping cream

Segments from 5 oranges for garnish

Preheat oven to 400°.

Cut the butter into the flour using a pastry blender or two blunt-edged knives. Stir in 2 tablespoons of the sugar and mix with just enough water to bind the dough; roll out with a rolling pin and line a 9-inch pie pan with dough. Prick the bottom of the dough with a fork and chill for 30 minutes. Line crust with greaseproof waxed paper, fill with pinto beans, and bake for 15 minutes. Then discard the paper and beans and bake for 10 minutes more. Remove from the oven and allow to cool.

In a bowl, combine the flour, remaining 4 tablespoons of sugar, cocoa, vanilla, grated orange zest and juice, egg yolks, and chile powder until smooth, adding a little of the milk if necessary. Heat the remaining milk in a saucepan, pour onto the paste and stir well. Pour the mixture into a saucepan and bring to a boil, stirring well all the time. Reduce the heat, simmer for 3 minutes, then remove from the heat and cover the surface of the sauce with dampened waxed paper. Allow to cool. Chill.

Brush the melted chocolate inside the cooked flan crust. Whip half the cream and fold it into the chilled filling. Spread the filling over the melted chocolate and chill well, about an hour. Whip the remaining cream and pipe equally spaced lines across the top of the flan. Arrange the orange segments in the gaps between the lines of cream just before serving. Cut and serve with a triangular spatula.

CUSTARD BAKING HINTS

• To test a baked custard for doneness, insert a dinner knife halfway between the edge and the center. If the knife comes out clean, the custard's done. The center will be jiggly, but will firm as it cools.

• A custard that "weeps" (oozes liquid) has been baked too long or at too high a temperature.

• Baked custards can be served hot, warm, or chilled.

—*Sharon Tyler Herbst*

RASPBERRY CREME BRÛLÉE
WITH JALAPEÑO VODKA

Yield: 6 servings
Heat Scale: Mild

Cooking the custard on the stove—rather than baking it—produces an especially soft and creamy texture. This recipe is courtesy of James B. O'Malley, who frequently reviews books for Chile Pepper *magazine. Note: This recipe requires advance preparation.*

- 1 (12-ounce) package frozen unsweetened raspberries, thawed, drained
- $3/4$ cup granulated sugar
- 2 teaspoons Jalapeño Vodka (page 159)
- 5 egg yolks
- 2 cups whipping cream
- $1/4$ teaspoon vanilla extract
- 5 teaspoons unsalted butter
- $1/3$ cup firmly packed brown sugar

In a bowl, mix the berries with $1/4$ cup of the sugar and the vodka. Divide the berries among six $3/4$-cup broilerproof ramekins or custard cups. Whisk the egg yolks and remaining $1/2$ cup sugar in a heavy, medium saucepan until pale and thick, about 3 minutes. Add the cream and vanilla and mix well.

Place the saucepan over medium heat and stir until the custard thickens, about 7 minutes. Do not boil. Add the butter and stir until melted. Spoon this mixture over the berries. Cover and refrigerate at least 4 hours or overnight.

Preheat the broiler. Press the brown sugar through a sieve over the custards. Broil until the sugar begins to melt and caramelize, about 2 minutes. Chill for 3 hours before serving.

CHILE AND SPICE
PUMPKIN PUDDING

Yield: 10 servings

Heat Scale: Mild

Like a pie without the crust, this pudding is for pumpkin lovers who like a little chile, too. Why not serve this for Thanksgiving dinner?

3 cups half-and-half

6 large eggs

$^{1}/_{2}$ cup granulated sugar

$^{1}/_{2}$ cup firmly packed light brown sugar

6 tablespoons unsulfured (light) molasses

$1^{1}/_{2}$ teaspoons ground cinnamon

$1^{1}/_{2}$ teaspoons ground ginger

$^{3}/_{4}$ teaspoon ground nutmeg

$^{1}/_{8}$ teaspoon ground cloves

1 teaspoon New Mexican red chile powder

$^{1}/_{4}$ teaspoon salt

1 ($1^{1}/_{2}$-pound) can solid pack pumpkin

Preheat oven to 325°. Butter a shallow 8-cup baking dish.

Bring the half-and-half to simmer in small saucepan, then set it aside. In a large bowl, combine the eggs, both sugars, molasses, cinnamon, ginger, nutmeg, cloves, chile powder, and salt in large bowl and beat well to blend. Add the pumpkin and warm half-and-half and mix well.

Pour mixture into the baking dish, and set the dish in a hot water bath. Bake until the custard is set and a knife inserted 2 inches from the center comes out clean, about 50 minutes. Cool completely. Serve at room temperature or cover and refrigerate.

NEW MEXICO BREAD PUDDING
WITH CHIMAYÓ CHILE

Yield: 10 to 12 servings

Heat Scale: Medium

Here's a Southwestern twist on bread pudding. The tequila, bolillo rolls, red chile, pine nuts, and pecans are part of the familiar flavors of New Mexico. We prefer Chimayó red chile, a hot chile from the northern part of the state. Why not serve it with New Mexican Hot Chocolate (page 158)? Note: This recipe requires advance preparation.

1 cup raisins

$^1/_4$ cup tequila

11 ounces day-old bolillo rolls or French bread, cut into $^1/_2$-inch pieces (about 11 cups)

$2^1/_2$ cups whipping cream

$2^1/_2$ cups smooth applesauce

$1^1/_3$ cups granulated sugar

6 tablespoons unsalted butter, melted

3 large eggs

1 teaspoon ground cinnamon

$^1/_2$ teaspoon ground nutmeg

2 teaspoons New Mexican Chimayó red chile powder

$1^1/_3$ cups chopped pecans

1 cup pine nuts

Vanilla ice cream or one of the ice creams in Chapter 10

Combine raisins and tequila in small bowl. Marinate for 1 hour. Remove and drain the raisins.

Preheat oven to 350°. Generously butter 11 by 9 by 2-inch baking pan, and place the bread in the pan. In a large bowl, combine the cream, applesauce, sugar, butter, eggs, cinnamon, nutmeg, and red chile and whisk to blend. Add the marinated raisins, pecans, and pine nuts. Pour over bread in pan. Cover the pan with aluminum foil. Bake until the center of the pudding is firm, about 1 hour. Cool slightly. Spoon the pudding into bowls and top with the ice cream.

SPICY SWEET POTATO PONE

Yield: 8 servings
Heat Scale: Medium

We don't normally think of sweet potatoes in a pudding, but they work well in this Trinidadian recipe that we have spiced up. This is one of the few pudding recipes that does not require a water bath.

1 pound raw sweet potatoes, grated (about 3 cups)

1 cup coconut milk

$1^{1}/_{4}$ cups loosely packed brown sugar

1 teaspoon ground ginger

$^{1}/_{2}$ teaspoon habanero powder

$^{1}/_{4}$ teaspoon ground cinnamon

1 teaspoon vanilla extract

$^{1}/_{2}$ teaspoon ground nutmeg

$^{1}/_{4}$ cup raisins

$^{1}/_{4}$ cup thinly sliced orange zest

1 tablespoon unsweetened shredded coconut

2 cups hot water

2 tablespoons melted butter

Allspice for garnish

Preheat the oven to 350°. Grease a large baking dish.

In a bowl, combine the grated sweet potatoes with the coconut milk, brown sugar, ginger, habanero powder, cinnamon, vanilla, and nutmeg and mix well. Add the remaining ingredients and taste for desired sweetness, adding more brown sugar if you wish. Mix well and pour the mixture into the prepared baking dish and bake for 1 hour. Remove, cool to room temperature, and sprinkle with the allspice.

BREAD PUDDING WITH CHOCOLATE AND CHILE POWDER

Yield: 6 to 8 servings

Heat Scale: Medium

Our friend Jasmine DeLuisa, of Las Vegas, graciously contributed this recipe. She suggests serving the pudding with espresso.

1 (8-ounce) French baguette, cut into $^1/_4$-inch-thick rounds

$^1/_2$ cup unsalted butter, melted

3 cups whipping cream

1 cup milk

8 large egg yolks

2 large eggs

$^1/_2$ cup granulated sugar

1 tablespoon vanilla extract

Pinch of salt

$^1/_2$ teaspoon habanero or chiltepin powder

8 ounces bittersweet or semisweet chocolate, chopped, melted in a double boiler

Whipped cream for garnish

Ground allspice for garnish

Arrange the bread slices on a large baking sheet. Brush with melted butter. Bake until crisp, about 15 minutes. Remove from the oven and cool.

Heat 3 cups of cream and the milk in a medium saucepan over medium heat until just warm to touch. Whisk the yolks, eggs, sugar, vanilla, salt, and chile powder in a bowl. Gradually whisk in the warm cream mixture.

Place the melted chocolate in a large bowl. Gradually whisk in the cream mixture until well blended. Stand the bread slices on their sides in a 9-inch round cake pan with 2-inch high sides. Pour the chocolate custard over the bread and let stand until the bread softens and absorbs some of the custard, while pressing the bread down occasionally, about 40 minutes. Meanwhile, preheat oven to 350°.

Place the cake pan in a hot water bath. Bake until a knife inserted in the center of the pudding comes out clean, about 1 hour. Cool slightly. To serve, spoon the pudding into dishes, top with a dollop of whipped cream and a sprinkle of allspice.

SHIR BIRINJ
(AFGHANI RICE PUDDING)

Yield: 6 servings
Heat Scale: Medium

This recipe is adapted from one by Dr. Arnold Krochmal, who lived in Afghanistan during the 1950s. In an article for Chile Pepper *he wrote, "This is a favorite desert, using the ever-present rice. The vanilla essence is sometimes omitted in villages where it may not be available."*

2 cups cooked rice

$1^{1}/_{4}$ cups milk

$^{1}/_{8}$ teaspoon salt

$^{1}/_{2}$ cup loosely packed brown sugar

1 tablespoon butter or margarine

1 teaspoon vanilla extract

2 eggs, beaten

$^{1}/_{2}$ cup raisins

$^{1}/_{2}$ teaspoon cayenne powder

Chopped pistachios for garnish

Combine all ingredients except the pistachios and place in a greased baking dish. Bake at 300° for about 45 minutes. Garnish with pistachios and serve.

NAWLINS CAYENNE BREAD PUDDING
WITH CHANTILLY CREAM

Yield: 8 servings

Heat Scale: Medium

Fair is fair, so let's give another hot spot a chance at a spicy bread pudding. That's New Orleans, of course, with cayenne as the hot spice of choice. This recipe takes forever, but is well worth it!

$^{1}/_{2}$ cup raisins

1 cup warm water

1 teaspoon lemon juice

5 cups cubed bread, very stale

3 large eggs

1 cup honey

1 teaspoon fresh grated nutmeg

1 teaspoons ground cinnamon

$^{1}/_{2}$ teaspoon cayenne powder, or more to taste

Pinch of salt

$1^{1}/_{2}$ teaspoons vanilla extract

2 teaspoons brandy

$^{1}/_{4}$ cup melted butter

$2^{1}/_{2}$ cups milk

$^{1}/_{2}$ cup chopped pecans

CHANTILLY CREAM

$^{2}/_{3}$ cup heavy cream

1 teaspoon vanilla extract

2 tablespoons granulated sugar

2 tablespoons sour cream

Combine the raisins, warm water, and lemon juice in a small bowl and marinate for at least 30 minutes.

Place a bowl and the beaters of an electric mixer in the freezer. Preheat oven to 350°. Grease an 11 by 8-inch cake pan.

In a large bowl, beat the eggs with electric mixer on high until frothy, about 3 minutes (not with chilled beaters). Add the honey, nutmeg, cinnamon, cayenne, salt, vanilla, brandy, and butter and beat until well blended. Beat in milk, then stir in drained raisins and pecans.

Place the bread cubes in the prepared loaf pan, pour egg mixture over, and toss until the bread is soaked. Let sit for about 45 minutes, occasionally patting the bread down into the liquid. Place in the oven, lower heat to 300°, and bake for 45 minutes. Increase the oven temperature to 425° and bake until pudding is brown and puffy, about 15 to 20 minutes more.

Right before the bread pudding is done, prepare the Chantilly Cream. Combine the cream, vanilla extract, brandy, sugar, and sour cream in the refrigerated bowl and beat with the cold beaters until soft peaks form, about 3 minutes.

Remove the bread pudding from the oven and allow it to cool for 10 minutes. To serve, spoon $^1/_2$ cup warm bread pudding onto dessert plates and top with a spoonful of Chantilly Cream.

RICE PUDDING WITH COCONUT-HABANERO-MANGO TOPPING

Yield: 8 to 10 servings
Heat Scale: Medium

This tropical dessert should be served with Burning Brandy Alexanders (page 167). Nondrinkers can have a cappucino.

6 eggs, beaten

$1^1/_2$ cups cooked white rice

$^1/_4$ teaspoon salt

$^1/_2$ cup granulated sugar

2 teaspoons vanilla extract

$1^1/_2$ teaspoons grated lemon zest

$3^1/_2$ cups milk

2 cups sliced fresh mangoes

1 tablespoon freshly squeezed lemon juice

2 tablespoons brandy

$^1/_4$ habanero chile, puréed with a little water

1 cup shredded sweetened coconut

Preheat oven to 350°. Lightly butter a 2-quart baking dish.

In a bowl, combine the eggs with the rice, salt, sugar, vanilla, lemon zest, and milk, and mix well. Pour into the baking dish. Set the dish in a hot water bath. Bake for 1 hour, or until the pudding is set. Remove from the oven and cool.

Meanwhile, combine the mangoes, lemon juice, brandy, habanero, and coconut in a bowl; cover and chill for 2 hours. To serve, spoon the chilled mangoes on top of the cooled pudding.

4

▲▲▲▲▲▲▲▲▲▲▲▲▲▲▲▲▲▲▲▲▲▲▲▲▲▲▲▲▲▲▲▲▲▲▲▲

BOLD BREADS &
SPICED CRUMBLES

Bread, and the flours used to create it, have been a mainstay of nutrition from almost the beginning of time. Throughout the world, flour was consumed early on, mostly in the form of porridge, mush, and gruel. However, it seems as if the Greeks livened things up by creating the true art of baking. In the third century, the Greek Athenaeus, listed at least 72 different kinds of bread, each with an established definition.

Bread has also served in religious rituals, from the Christian sacrament wafer to the matza of the Jews, and has even been viewed as a religious icon. Throughout many periods of history, whole populations survived war and famine on little more than bread and water—it is definitely a sustainer of life.

But according to *History of Foods*, it is the Egyptians whom we should credit for creating baking techniques that were both creative and predictable. If only the tombs could talk! We wonder what those culinarily creative Egyptians would think of our hot and sweet breads and crisps.

Let's begin with a few recipes that would surely make them proud and that are certainly creative contributions to breakfast, lunch, or after-dinner events. Thankfully, cookies were transformed from dried-out biscuits to their current fabulous form many years ago; we honor them with a plethora of peppers.

Coffee isn't just for breakfast anymore. With the addition of literally thousands of coffee houses all over the country, which, by the way, are just as likely to serve more coffee in the evening than in the morning, new desserts needed to be created to fill the late-night time slot! As you might have guessed, we've come up with a few that we think fit the bill. And finally, we've turned up the heat with some scintillating cookies.

JUMPIN' JALAPEÑO CORN MUFFINS WITH CHILE-ORANGE BUTTER

Yield: 24
Heat Scale: Medium

This is a great recipe for those times you've run out of jelly and need a sweet heat fix. We like to make a little extra Chile-Orange Butter to save for sautéing fish and vegetables.

4 jalapeño chiles, stemmed, seeded, and finely chopped

2 cups milk

1 cup buttermilk

3 eggs

1 cup cornmeal

$3/_4$ cup flour

4 tablespoons granulated sugar

3 tablespoons baking powder

$1^1/_2$ teaspoons salt

Preheat the oven to 375°.

Mix the chiles, milk, buttermilk, and eggs. Sift together dry ingredients and add to the liquid. Mix them quickly, making certain to combine the batter completely.

Pour batter into greased muffin tins, about one-half full. Bake for 20 to 30 minutes or until done. Serve warm with Chile-Orange Butter.

CHILE-ORANGE BUTTER

1 tablespoon New Mexican red chile powder

$1/_2$ tablespoon grated orange zest

$1/_2$ tablespoon grated lemon zest

2 teaspoons orange juice

1 pound butter, softened

Combine all ingredients and allow to sit at room temperature for an hour to blend the flavors.

STRAWBERRY-ANCHO BLUE CORN MUFFINS

Yield: 12 to 15
Heat Scale: Medium

These muffins need not be served at breakfast only. They complement almost any dinner or luncheon, and of course they can always be served as dessert.

1 cup flour
$3/4$ cup blue cornmeal
$1/3$ cup granulated sugar
3 teaspoons baking powder
$3/4$ teaspoons salt
2 teaspoons ancho chile powder
1 cup finely chopped strawberries, washed and hulled
1 cup milk
1 egg, beaten
2 tablespoons melted butter or margarine

Preheat oven to 425°.

Sift together dry ingredients. In a separate bowl, combine strawberries, milk, egg, and butter. Pour the dry ingredients into the wet ingredients and mix well. Lightly grease a muffin pan, and pour the batter into the cups, about one-half full. Bake for 15 to 20 minutes.

JAMANERO
OAT MUFFINS

Yield: 12

Heat Scale: Hot

A tingly combination of peach preserves and habaneros make these the most wonderful muffins around. If you're truly adventurous, you can add a little Habanero Peach Preserves from our friends at Stonewall Chili Pepper Company or one of our hot and spicy preserves or jams in Chapter 5 to really give these muffins some zing.

- 1 cup quick-cooking (not instant) oats
- 1 cup buttermilk
- 1 large egg, beaten to blend
- $^1/_2$ cup butter, melted
- $^1/_2$ teaspoon habanero powder
- 1 cup all-purpose flour
- $^1/_2$ cup firmly packed brown sugar
- 2 teaspoons baking powder
- 1 teaspoon baking soda
- $^1/_2$ teaspoon salt
- $^1/_4$ cup peach preserves

Preheat oven to 350°. Lightly grease two 6-cup muffin tins.

Combine oats and buttermilk in a medium bowl, and let stand for 2 minutes. Next, stir in the egg and butter. In a separate bowl, mix the habanero powder, flour, brown sugar, baking powder, baking soda, and salt. Combine the dry mixture to the oat mixture, and stir until it is just combined. Divide batter equally among the cups. Top each with 1 teaspoon jam. Bake the muffins until a toothpick inserted into the centers comes out clean, about 18 minutes. Turn the muffins out onto a wire rack. Cool slightly and serve.

HIGHLY SPICED
PUMPKIN ROLLS

Yield: 12

Heat Scale: Medium

Buy an extra pumpkin at Halloween, or better yet, grow a few so you'll have a fresh supply of this New World crop. This highly regarded member of the gourd family eagerly takes on the heat of the chile to produce rolls that you'll want to make over and over.

$^2/_3$ cup milk

1 cup cooked mashed pumpkin or canned pumpkin

2 tablespoons orange zest

2 tablespoons New Mexican red chile powder

$^1/_3$ cup firmly packed brown sugar

$^1/_2$ teaspoon salt

$^1/_3$ cup butter or margarine

1 package yeast dissolved in $^1/_4$ cup warm water

4 to 5 cups whole-wheat flour

1 cup raisins

Preheat the oven to 400°. Grease two 6-cup muffin tins. Scald the milk and allow it to cool.

Combine the pumpkin, orange zest, chile, sugar, salt, and butter and mix well. Add the yeast mixture, 2 cups of flour, and raisins, then beat well. Gradually stir in more flour until the dough is stiff enough to be kneaded. Knead on a floured board until the dough is smooth and elastic.

Place the dough in a buttered bowl, cover with a clean towel, and let rise until doubled. When the dough has doubled, punch it down and turn it onto a floured board. Divide the dough into 12 equal portions. Place each portion into prepared muffin tins, then cover and let the dough rise until it doubles.

Bake the rolls for 20 minutes, or until golden brown. Brush the rolls with soft butter while they are hot.

BANANA, ANCHO, AND
MACADAMIA NUT MUFFINS

Yield: 12

Heat Scale: Medium

*Believe it or not, the macadamia nut tree was first grown only for orna-
mental purposes. Thankfully, someone experimented with the nuts and
discovered their butterlike, slightly sweet nature. This bread is so rich
you won't need to butter it. We like to serve it as a late night snack
with hot tea.*

$1^1/_2$ cups unbleached all-purpose flour

$1^1/_2$ teaspoons baking soda

$^1/_4$ teaspoon salt

$^1/_8$ teaspoon ground nutmeg

$^1/_8$ teaspoon ground ginger

$1^1/_4$ cups mashed ripe bananas (about 3 large)

3 teaspoons lemon zest

2 pasilla or ancho chiles, stemmed, seeded,
   and chopped

$^1/_2$ cup granulated sugar

$^1/_4$ cup firmly packed dark brown sugar

1 stick butter, softened

$^1/_4$ cup milk

1 large egg

1 cup unsalted macadamia nuts, toasted, chopped

Preheat oven to 350°. Grease two 6-cup muffin tins.

Sift the flour, baking soda, salt, nutmeg, and ginger into a large bowl.
In a separate bowl, combine the bananas, lemon zest, pasillas, sugars, butter, milk, and eggs. Mix the wet mixture into the dry ingredients. Next,
fold in half of the nuts.

Divide the batter equally among prepared muffin tins. Sprinkle the tops
of muffins with the remaining macadamia nuts. Bake for about 25 minutes

or until the muffins are golden brown, and a toothpick inserted into their centers comes out clean. Transfer muffins to a wire rack and cool.

BANANA BREAD
WITH A BITE

Yield: 1 loaf

Heat Scale: Medium

Never despair over blackened banana again. In fact, this bread is so good and easy you may even find yourself buying extra bananas in hopes that a few will get overripe. This bread is also delicious when accompanied by the White Chocolate-Ancho Chile Ice Cream (page 184).

1 cup firmly packed dark brown sugar

$^1/_2$ cup butter or margarine

2 eggs

$^1/_2$ cup green chile, roasted, stemmed, seeded, and chopped

$1^1/_2$ cups mashed ripe bananas

2 cups plus 2 tablespoons flour

2 teaspoons baking powder

$^1/_2$ teaspoon salt

$^1/_2$ cup chopped pecans or walnuts

$^1/_2$ cup semisweet chocolate chips (optional)

Preheat the oven to 350°.

Cream brown sugar and margarine until fluffy. Add the eggs, one at a time, beating the mixture well after each addition. Stir in the chile and mix well. Fold in the bananas. Combine the dry ingredients and add to the mixture. Mix in the nuts. Pour the mixture into a greased 9 by 5-inch loaf pan. If using the chocolate chips, sprinkle on top. Bake for 1 hour 10 minutes, or until a toothpick inserted in the center comes out clean.

Allow to cool for 15 minutes before removing from pan. Cool completely before slicing.

ETHIOPIAN AMBASHA

Yield: 8

Heat Scale: Medium

This fiery, sweet spice bread, from Chile Pepper magazine, is baked in a pizza pan. Several Ethiopian breads incorporate berbere, which is a hot pepper seasoning, whether mixed in the actual bread dough or spread on top, as in this recipe. This simplified version uses a quick berbere substitute, but any berbere seasoning can be substituted. Fenugreek seeds may be found in any Asian market and from mail-order spice companies.

1 tablespoon active dry yeast

$^1/_4$ cup warm water

2 tablespoons ground coriander

1 teaspoon ground cardamom

$^1/_2$ teaspoon white pepper

1 teaspoon ground fenugreek

2 teaspoons salt

$^1/_3$ cup vegetable oil

$1^1/_4$ cups lukewarm water

5 cups unbleached flour

TOPPING

1 tablespoon cayenne powder

2 tablespoons vegetable oil

$^1/_4$ teaspoon ground ginger

Pinch of ground cloves

$^1/_8$ teaspoon ground cinnamon

Preheat the oven to 350°.

Dissolve yeast in warm water and let proof for 10 minutes. Add the coriander, cardamom, white pepper, fenugreek, salt, oil, and lukewarm water, and stir well. Slowly add the flour until a mass forms. On a floured board, knead the dough for 10 minutes or until it is smooth and tiny bubbles form. (The dough should be unusually sticky.) Reserve a 1-inch piece of dough.

With floured hands, spread the dough out on an ungreased 12-inch pizza pan. Using a sharp knife, score the dough in a design similar to the spokes of a bicycle wheel. Place the reserved ball of dough in the center of the scored dough. Cover and let rise for 1 hour. Bake at 350° for 1 hour or until golden brown. Combine the topping ingredients in a small bowl. While still warm, brush the bread with the topping.

AND YOU THINK BIG BROTHER'S WATCHING NOW ...

In the year 1202, England enacted her first laws to regulate the price of bread and limit the amount of profit a baker may earn.

PASILLA SCONES WITH
RED CHILE HONEY

Yield: 16

Heat Scale: Medium

These tender flaky scones are best served warm from the oven. The pasilla chile adds a little bit of heat and a really nice raisiny taste. We recommend serving these for breakfast with Red Chile Honey or raspberry preserves. (Unused Red Chile Honey can be stored at room temperature.) Cut out the scones with a heart- or chile-shaped cookie cutter, and you've got the beginnings of a great day.

   2 cups all-purpose flour

   1 teaspoon salt

   1 tablespoon baking powder

   $^1/_3$ cup finely chopped dried and seeded pasilla chiles

   1 teaspoon cinnamon

   1 cup plus 2 tablespoons whipping cream

Preheat oven to 425°.

In a large bowl, mix together the flour, salt, and baking powder. Add the chile, cinnamon, and 1 cup of the cream and stir until a soft dough forms. Place the dough on a floured surface and knead 10 times, or until the mixture forms a ball.

Divide dough into 2 pieces. Roll out on a floured surface to about $^1/_2$ inch thick, then cut out the scones using a cookie cutter, and place them on a baking sheet. Brush the tops of each scone with the remaining 2 tablespoons of cream. Bake for 15 minutes or until golden brown.

RED CHILE HONEY

   1 tablespoon New Mexican red chile powder

   1 (8-ounce) jar commercial honey

Mix the red chile powder into the honey. Serve with scones. Store at room temperature.

SERRANO-ZUCCHINI
CARROT BREAD

Yield: 2 loaves

Heat Scale: Medium

If you are like Melissa, zucchini are one of the few things that you can always count on coming out in full force when you plant a garden. We like this moist bread because it is the perfect way to get rid of a few zucchini and to make friends with new neighbors.

3 eggs

1 cup vegetable oil

$2^1/_2$ cups sugar

1 cup grated zucchini

1 cup grated carrots

$2^1/_2$ teaspoons vanilla extract

2 serrano or jalapeño chiles, stemmed, seeded, and minced

3 cups all-purpose flour

1 teaspoon salt

$^1/_2$ teaspoon baking powder

3 teaspoons ground cinnamon

$^1/_2$ cup chopped nuts

Preheat oven to 350°.

In a large bowl, beat the eggs. Next, add the oil, sugar, zucchini, carrots, vanilla, and serranos. Combine the dry ingredients in a separate bowl, then slowly add the dry mixture to the zucchini mixture, mixing well. Stir in the nuts. Pour the batter into 2 greased loaf pans and bake for 1 hour. Make sure you do not overbake, or the bread will be dry.

BOLD BAKLAVA

Yield: 40
Heat Scale: Medium

This is a Greek dessert that has gone where no Greek dessert has ever gone before! Of course, we are referring to the red chile, which truly makes this a dessert to remember. You may want to make your own phyllo dough for this recipe, but we prefer to use the time-saving commercial type, which tastes great and can be found in the frozen foods section of your grocery store. For best results, thaw the phyllo in the refrigerator, and keep a moist towel over the leaves as you work with them to prevent the dough from drying out.

4 cups ground walnuts

$^1/_2$ cup granulated sugar

Ground cinnamon to taste

1 cup melted sweet butter

10 to 15 sheets phyllo dough, thawed and covered with a
damp kitchen towel

SYRUP

1 cup honey

2 cups cold water

2 cups granulated sugar

A few lemon or orange rinds

1 tablespoon New Mexican red chile powder

1 cinnamon stick

Preheat the oven to 350°.

In a large mixing bowl, combine the walnuts, sugar, and cinnamon, and mix well. Brush a baking sheet with melted butter. Place 2 phyllo leaves at the bottom of the tray and brush with butter. Spread some of the nut mixture evenly over the leaves. Place 2 or more leaves on top. Again brush with the butter and repeat the layering procedure until the tray is filled. Place the last 3 leaves on top, brush with butter, and score the top sheets in square or diamond shapes with a pointed knife.

Bake for 30 minutes, then reduce the heat to 300° and bake for 45 minutes more or until the top becomes golden brown.

To make the syrup, mix all the ingredients in a saucepan and boil for 10 minutes. Allow to cool. When the pastry is cool, pour the syrup over the baklava. Cut into rectangular pieces and serve.

LUCKY NUMBER 13

Ever wonder why when you go to a bakery and purchase a dozen cookies or rolls, they throw in the thirteenth one for free? This tradition actually goes back to ancient Egypt, where bakers caught short-weighting were nailed to the door of their shops. In England, bakers caught doing the same thing were fined by government authorities. In order to avoid trouble, many bakers in both Egypt and England voluntarily threw in an extra cookie or bun just to guard against problems (or bodily injuries!).

PEAR AND
CRANBERRY-RED CHILE CRISP

Yield: 4 servings

Heat Scale: Medium

🔥 🔥

The red of the cranberry and chile makes this as pretty to look at as it is good to eat. We like to serve this dish in individual oven-safe bowls. It makes a great impression when each guest gets their own hot and sweet desert.

TOPPING

- 1 cup unbleached all-purpose flour
- $^2/_3$ cup firmly packed brown sugar
- $^1/_2$ cup old-fashioned oats
- $^1/_4$ teaspoon salt
- $^1/_2$ cup chilled unsalted butter, cut into pieces

FILLING

- 7 large firm ripe pears (about $3^1/_2$ pounds) peeled, cored, cut lengthwise into eighths
- 1 cup fresh frozen cranberries
- 3 teaspoons New Mexican red chile powder
- $^1/_2$ cup granulated sugar
- 2 tablespoons unbleached all-purpose flour
- $^1/_2$ teaspoon ground cinnamon
- $^1/_4$ teaspoon ground nutmeg

Combine the flour, brown sugar, oats, and salt in medium bowl. Add the butter and cut it in using a pastry blender or two blunt edged knives until the mixture resembles a coarse meal. Set aside.

Position a rack in the center of oven, and preheat oven to 350°. Butter 4 individual dessert bowls, and set aside.

In a large bowl, combine the pears, cranberries, chile powder, granulated sugar, flour, cinnamon, and nutmeg. Mix well. Transfer the fruit mixture to the individual bowls.

Sprinkle the topping evenly over the filling in each bowl. Set the bowls on a baking sheet and transfer to the oven. Bake until the topping is golden and juices are thick and bubbling, about 1 hour. Cool at least 20 minutes before serving.

TRIPLE-CHILE AND NECTARINE CRISP

Yield: 6 servings

Heat Scale: Hot

Three chiles are certainly better than one! Combine them with the sweet taste of the ripe nectarines, and lots of other interesting ingredients, and you've got a hot hit on your hands. Serve this with Ancho-Walnut Cream (page 186) for the truly hot at heart!

TOPPING

$3/4$ cup pine nuts

$1/3$ cup firmly packed light brown sugar

15 purchased gingersnaps, broken into pieces

2 teaspoons New Mexico red chile powder

1 cup quick-cooking oats

1 teaspoon ground ginger

$3/4$ teaspoon salt

$1/2$ cup plus 2 tablespoons chilled unsalted butter, cut into pieces

2 large egg yolks

5 tablespoons chopped crystallized ginger

FILLING

2 tablespoons lemon juice

4 pounds ripe nectarines (about 10)

1 teaspoon jalapeño powder

$1/2$ cup firmly packed light brown sugar

2 tablespoons cornstarch

1 large egg yolk

2 fresh chile pequins, stemmed, seeded, and minced

Preheat the oven to 375°. Butter a 13 by 9 by 2-inch baking dish, and set aside.

To make the topping, place the pine nuts with the brown sugar in a food processor and pulse until chopped. Add the gingersnaps and red chile, and process until coarsely chopped. Next, blend in the oats, ground ginger, and salt. Add the butter and cut in, pulsing until a coarse meal forms. Finally, add the yolks and crystallized ginger and process until all of the ingredients are combined, but the mixture is still chunky. Set aside.

Place the lemon juice in large bowl. Peel and pit the nectarines. Thinly slice them into the bowl; toss to coat with lemon juice. Mix in the jalapeño powder, brown sugar, cornstarch, yolk and pequins. Spoon the fruit mixture into the prepared dish.

Sprinkle the topping evenly over the nectarine filling. Bake until the topping is deep light brown, about 1 hour. Let the dessert cool at least 15 minutes.

5

SEARING JAMS
& JELLIES

One of the most popular chile products and most requested recipes at *Chile Pepper* magazine is pepper jelly—a sweet-heat favorite with hundreds of variations. We present six of those in this chapter, along with preserves, jams, marmalades, relishes, apple butter, and fruit chutneys.

Some of these delights are hard to tell apart. "Because jams, jellies, preserves, and marmalades are similar products," wrote Lynda Pozel in *Chile Pepper* magazine, "there's some confusion over what is what. Basically, jellies are made from strained juice; jams are a combination of juice and pulp; and preserves are like jams but usually have larger pieces of fruit. Marmalade, at least as most people know it today, is made of citrus fruits."

Since most people will make rather large quantities of the jams and jellies here (it's hard to make just 1 cup), cooks should be prepared. Some of the equipment needed includes a heavy 6- to-8-quart stockpot with a wide flat bottom, canning jars with seals and lids, measuring cups, a wooden spoon, and a wide-mouthed funnel. And follow this hint about jelly preparation, from Howard Hillman, a food writer who has studied the science of the kitchen: "Only a small quantity of this concentrate is necessary; beware of an overdose, which will give the jelly a tough, rubbery consistency."

There are basically two ways to store the jams and other recipes in this chapter: in clean jars or in sterilized jars. If you plan to consume the jam within a week or two, there's no need to sterilize the jars. Simply wash them and the lids and seals in a dishwasher. After filling the jars, store them in the refrigerator.

For longer storage, you should process the jars in a boiling water bath. Place the jars (mouth side down), the lids, and the seals in a large

Pine Nut Flan with Red Chile Caramel Sauce

Pasilla Scones

pan or canning kettle, pour boiling water over them until the water is 2 inches deep, cover the pan, and boil for 15 minutes. Remove the jars, lids, and seals with sterile tongs, allow them to dry for a few minutes, and then fill with the jam and seal. Some recipes call for the jam-filled jars to be processed again in a boiling water bath to further sterilize them. Preserving expert Loni Kuhn notes, "The high sugar content of jams, jellies, and chutneys eliminates the necessity of processing them further in a water bath, but this does help assure a good seal." Some sources suggest that the nearly filled jars be covered with a layer of paraffin before sealing, to prevent mold from growing. In addition, Lynda Pozel advises, "Do not double recipes. Instead, make several batches." (For more information about canning, refer to *Keeping the Harvest* by Nancy Chioffi and Gretchen Mead.)

PINEAPPLE-LEMON-APPLE
PRESERVES WITH HABANERO

Yield: 3 cups

Heat Scale: Hot

Serve these preserves with hot croissants and strong, rich coffee. They also can be served slightly warm over vanilla ice cream—or (heh, heh) any of the ice creams in Chapter 10.

$2^1/_2$ cups coarsely chopped pineapple (1 small pineapple)

$1^1/_2$ cups coarsely chopped apples

1 habanero chile, stemmed, seeded, and finely chopped

$^1/_2$ cup quartered lemon slices

3 cups granulated sugar

3 tablespoons brandy or cognac

Place the pineapple, apples, and habanero into a large pot and cook over low heat for 10 minutes, stirring occasionally. While the apples and pineapple are cooking, bring a small pot of water to a high boil, turn off the heat, and add the lemon. After 5 minutes, drain the lemon. Add the blanched lemon and the sugar to the pineapple and apple mixture. Cook over low heat for $1^1/_2$ hours, skimming off foam as necessary.

Pour into 3 sterilized half-pint jars and add 1 tablespoon of brandy to each jar.

BAKED AND SPICED
RASPBERRY PRESERVES

Yield: About 3 cups
Heat Scale: Mild

The simple technique of baking the raspberries was inspired by the writings of English author Elizabeth David, one of the finest food writers of the century. "This is by far the best raspberry jam I have ever tasted," she wrote. "It preserves almost intact the fresh flavour of the fruit, and will keep for a year." Of course, we suggest adding red chile powder to spice it up.

3 cups raspberries (about 1 pound)

2 cups granulated sugar

2 teaspoons New Mexican red chile powder

Preheat oven to 350°.

Place the raspberries and sugar in separate ovenproof bowls and place them in the oven. Bake for 25 minutes.

Combine the raspberries, sugar, and chile powder in a bowl and mix them well with a spoon. Fill 3 sterilized half-pint jars with the mixture and seal.

**GIFTS FIT FOR A QUEEN
(YOUR RELATIVES SHOULD
APPRECIATE 'EM TOO)**

According to History of Food, sugars and preserves were once gifts valued even by monarchs. When Charlotte of Savoy, the wife of Louis XI, visited Paris for the first time in 1467, she was presented with a heart made of preserves.

RED CHILE-BLUEBERRY JAM

Yield: About thirteen 4-ounce jars
Heat Scale: Mild

Fresh blueberries make a terrific jam, and the red chile powder spices it up just enough. Try this over scones or any other bread. It's also great over waffles.

1$^1/_2$ quarts fresh blueberries

2 tablespoons fresh lemon juice

1 (.75-ounce) packet powdered pectin

4 cups granulated sugar

2 tablespoons New Mexican red chile powder

Put blueberries in a large saucepan, crush with a wooden spoon and add the lemon juice and powdered pectin. Mix well and place over high heat. Bring the mixture to a hard boil and boil for 1 minute then stir in sugar and chile powder. Bring to a full rolling boil and boil hard 1 minute, stirring constantly. Remove from heat, stir, and skim off any foam with a large spoon. Cool for about 5 minutes and pour into hot, sterilized 4-ounce jars. Seal at once.

A BRIEF HISTORY OF PECTIN

"Most jams today are set with commercial pectin. Although pectin was discovered by French chemist Henri Braconnot in 1825, it wasn't until 1921 that Robert Douglas, son of a Scottish marmalade and jelly manufacturer, developed a process for recycling the apple pomace left over from his cider vinegar business into liquid pectin. This new business was so successful that he converted his entire plant to pectin manufacturing, and today's liquid and dry pectins are manufactured similarly to Douglas' original process.

"Commercial pectin was welcomed wholeheartedly by both commercial and home jelly-makers because it shortened the process, produced more reliable results, and made it possible to jell low-pectin fruits and even some vegetables, including peppers. Our grandmothers were not so lucky; they had to rely on trial and error and the experience of previous generations to tell them which fruits had enough natural pectin to set jams and jellies."

—Lynda Pozel

RED JALAPEÑO-APRICOT JELLY

Yield: Six $^1/_2$-pint jars
Heat Scale: Hot ⚘ ⚘ ⚘

Another great jelly from Nancy Gerlach calls for apricots, but dried peaches or nectarines work equally well. When this recipe appeared in Chile Pepper, she noted, "Any fresh green chile can be substituted depending on your heat preference. Serranos will make it hotter; roasted and peeled New Mexican chiles will tame it down."

- $^1/_2$ cup red jalapeño chiles, stemmed and seeded
- 1 large red bell pepper, stemmed and seeded
- 2 cups cider vinegar
- $1^1/_2$ cups chopped dried apricots
- 6 cups granulated sugar
- 3 ounces liquid pectin
- 3 to 4 drops red food color (optional)

Place the chiles, bell pepper, and vinegar in a blender and purée until coarsely ground and small chunks remain.

Combine the apricots, sugar, and chile mixture in a large saucepan, bring to a boil, and boil rapidly for 5 minutes. Remove from the heat and skim off any foam that forms. Allow the mixture to cool for 2 minutes and then mix in the pectin and food coloring. Pour into sterilized $^1/_2$-pint jars, seal, and cool.

JUMPIN' JALAPEÑO MARMALADE

Yield: Eight 4-ounce jars
Heat Scale: Medium

Chile Pepper writer Lynda Pozel also contributed this marmalade, which is similar to a relish with its chunks of red and green bell peppers and raisins, spiced just right with cinnamon, cloves, and allspice. Lynda suggests serving it as an accompaniment to pork, beef, or poultry, instead of reserving it for only toast and muffins.

4 oranges

3 quarts water

1 (3-inch) piece cinnamon stick, broken into pieces

1 teaspoon whole cloves

1 teaspoon whole allspice

1 lemon, thinly sliced, then chopped

2 green bell peppers, stemmed, seeded, and finely chopped

2 red bell peppers, stemmed, seeded, and finely chopped

3 cups granulated sugar

1 cup golden raisins

1 cup water

$^{1}/_{4}$ cup chopped jalapeño chiles

Peel the oranges, removing most of the white pith from the peel. Cut the peel into very thin strips. Cover the peel with $1^{1}/_{2}$ quarts of water, bring to a boil, and cook for 5 minutes; drain. Repeat with another $1^{1}/_{2}$ quarts water.

Remove the seeds and membranes from the orange pulp and chop; place in a heavy saucepan. Tie the cinnamon, cloves, and allspice in a square of cheesecloth and add to the saucepan along with the cooked orange peel, lemon, bell peppers, sugar, raisins and add 1 cup water. Cook over low heat until the sugar dissolves, stirring frequently. Bring to a boil and boil for 5 minutes. Cover and let stand at room temperature 1 hour to blend flavors. Bring back to a rolling boil and cook 10 minutes, stirring occasionally. Add the jalapeños and cook, stirring frequently, until the marmalade has thickened, about another 20 minutes. Remove and discard cheesecloth bag.

Spoon the marmalade into hot, sterilized 4-ounce jars leaving $^1/_4$ inch at the top. Wipe the rims with a clean towel, cover with canning jar lids and rings and process in a boiling water bath.

RED AND GREEN HOLIDAY JELLY

Yield: 6 cups
Heat Scale: Hot

From Chile Pepper food editor Nancy Gerlach comes a jelly that reflects the color of the season. "You can add some crushed chile if you want more heat or red color," she notes. "Serve this jelly as a canapé with cream cheese and crackers or as an accompaniment to beef, lamb, or pork."

$^3/_4$ cup chopped bell pepper
1 cup chopped red bell pepper
$^3/_4$ cup finely chopped jalapeño chiles
$1^1/_2$ cups cider vinegar
$6^1/_2$ cups granulated sugar
6 ounces liquid pectin

Place the bell peppers in a blender and grind, being careful not to grind the peppers too fine. Combine the ground peppers, chopped chiles, vinegar, and sugar, and bring to a rolling boil. Pour in the pectin, bring back to a rolling boil, and boil for 1 minute, stirring constantly. Remove from the heat and let sit for 1 minute and then skim off the foam. Pour into sterilized jars and seal.

FIERY BITTERSWEET ORANGE MARMALADE

Yield: Six $^1/_2$-pint jars

Heat Scale: Medium

Legend holds that this classic preserve originated when a cask of Seville oranges was lost at sea and washed up on the coast of Dundee, Scotland. Sea water had leaked into the barrel, partially pickling the oranges. The thrifty Scots, not wishing to waste the precious fruit, decided to preserve it with Scotch whisky. The only thing missing was the red jalapeño.

2 pounds bitter oranges (about 6)

2 quarts water

8 cups granulated sugar

1 red serrano or jalapeño chile, stemmed and seeded

Juice of 2 lemons

4 tablespoons Scotch whisky

Cut the oranges into quarters. Remove the seeds and reserve them. Scrape the pulp from the peel and reserve it. Tie the seeds in a piece of cheesecloth.

Shred the peel coarsely. Put the cheesecloth bag and the shredded peel in a saucepan and cover with 2 quarts water. Boil, covered, over medium heat for 1 hour. Remove the bag of seeds.

Warm the sugar by putting it in a cake pan and leaving it for 15 minutes in an oven preheated to its lowest setting. In a blender or food processor, purée the fruit pulp and jalapeños, and add it with the lemon juice and sugar to the pan of shredded peel. Stir over low heat until the sugar has dissolved, then increase the heat slightly and bring to a boil. Without stirring, boil for about 45 minutes until the marmalade sets.

Remove the pan from the heat and stir in the whisky immediately. Bottle in sterile $^1/_2$-pint preserving jars while still hot. Seal tightly.

FIVE-CITRUS, TWO-CHILE MARMALADE

Yield: About eight 1-pint jars
Heat Scale: Mild

Any combination of citrus fruit can be used in this recipe, as long as the total weight of the raw fruit is approximately half that of the sugar. Note: *This recipe requires advance preparation.*

- 2 grapefruits
- 2 lemons
- 2 limes
- 2 bitter oranges
- 2 tangerines
- 3 quarts plus 3 cups cold water
- $^1/_2$ cup green New Mexican chiles, roasted, stemmed, seeded, peeled, and finely chopped
- 2 jalapeño chiles, stemmed, seeded, and minced
- 12 cups granulated sugar

Peel the rinds off the fruit in thin strips with a potato peeler. Cut the peeled fruit into quarters, remove and reserve the seeds. Peel off the pith and put it with the seeds, cores, connective tissue, and the skin covering the grapefruit segments in a cheesecloth bag. Place the rinds, pulp, and cheesecloth bag in a large bowl, and add the water. Cover and leave for at least 24 hours.

Place the contents of the bowl in a large pan. Bring to a boil and simmer on very low heat until the rinds are very soft, about 2 hours. Remove the pan from the heat and remove the cheesecloth bag and discard. Return the pan to the heat and bring the liquid to a boil. Add the chiles and sugar, and remove the pan from the heat again. Stir with a wooden spoon until the sugar has dissolved. Return the pan to the heat and boil rapidly, without stirring, until the marmalade sets when tested, about 45 minutes. Remove the pan from the heat and let it stand 15 minutes. Pour into sterilized 1-pint jars, seal, and cool.

PINEAPPLE-DATIL JELLY

Yield: Six $^1/_2$-pint jars

Heat Scale: Hot

This interesting sweet-sour jelly recipe was handed down by the family of Mrs. Leonard Shugart of St. Augustine, Florida. It was first published in Chile Pepper *magazine.*

- 1 cup stemmed, seeded, and chopped datil peppers, or 3 stemmed, seeded, and chopped habaneros plus enough stemmed, seeded, and chopped red bell peppers to make 1 cup

- 2 cups cranberry juice

- 1 (16-ounce) can crushed pineapple in juice

- 1 tablespoon lemon juice

- 2 (.75-ounce) packets powdered pectin

- 3 cups granulated sugar

Place the peppers, cranberry juice, pineapple with juice, and lemon juice in blender or food processor and purée until smooth. Place the mixture in a large pot and add the pectin according to the directions on the package. Bring to a boil. Add sugar; bring to a hard rolling boil (do not stir). Boil 1 minute, skim off foam; fill sterilized $^1/_2$-pint jars and seal.

JELLY-MAKER'S TRICK

If your fruit jelly does not seem to be setting up correctly, place the jars in a shallow pan half-filled with cold water, then bake in a moderate oven for 30 minutes.

SCOTCH BONNET PEPPER JELLY

Yield: About 2 cups

Heat Scale: Extremely hot

From Jamaica comes this extremely hot and extremely sweet jelly that is served with pelaus *(stewed meats), roast pork, curry goat, baked chicken, and roasted lamb. Mixed with a little melted butter, it is transformed into a glaze for roasted pork or poultry.*

$^1/_4$ cup stemmed, seeded, and finely chopped
red and green Scotch bonnet or habanero chiles

$^1/_2$ cup stemmed, seeded, and finely chopped
green bell pepper

6 $^1/_2$ cups granulated sugar

1$^1/_2$ cups cider vinegar

6 ounces liquid pectin

Combine the Scotch bonnet, bell pepper, sugar, and vinegar in a saucepan and bring to a boil. Boil for 3$^1/_2$ minutes, stirring occasionally. Add the pectin and boil for 1$^1/_2$ minutes. Remove from heat and cool for 10 minutes and then pour into hot, sterilized jars.

MAXIMUM PECTIN

"Two main factors determine a jelly's pectin content. The first is the type of fruit used. For example, apples, citrus fruits, cranberries, sour blackberries, and quinces have a high pectin content. The opposite is true for apricots, pineapples, sour cherries, peaches, nectarines, raspberries, and strawberries. The second pectin-content determinant applies to all fruits: the stage of ripening. An almost ripe fruit is more appropriate for making jelly than a fully ripe or unripe one because useful pectin is at its maximum just before the fruit reaches its peak of ripeness."

—Howard Hillman

FRESH PEACH-HABANERO JELLY

Yield: About 4 cups

Heat Scale: Medium

🔥 🔥

We were inspired to make this jelly from the fresh peaches Jeff Camp-bell sends us every year from his farm in Stonewall, Texas. He also grows habaneros and manufactures a peach jam with them, so it seemed appropriate to turn the concept into a jelly. Serve this over corn bread, crackers (with cream cheese), or waffles.

$3^1/_2$ pounds fresh peaches (about 10), peeled and pitted

$^1/_2$ cup water

$^1/_4$ cup fresh lemon juice

$7^1/_2$ cups granulated sugar

1 habanero chile, stemmed, seeded, and puréed
with a little water

6 ounces liquid fruit pectin

Crush the peaches in a large saucepan with a wooden spoon and add the water. Heat to boiling point, reduce the heat and simmer, covered, for 5 minutes. Remove from the heat and cool to room temperature.

Place a large square of cheesecloth, several layers thick, in a colander set over a mixing bowl. Pour the peach mixture into cheesecloth, bring the corners together, and press tightly to extract all the liquid, about $3^1/_2$ cups. Return the juice back into the saucepan and add the lemon juice, sugar, and habanero. Heat to boiling, stirring constantly. Stir in the pectin, bring to a full rolling boil and boil hard for 1 minute, stirring constantly. Remove from the heat, skim off the foam, and pour quickly into sterilized jars. Seal at once.

CHILIED APPLE BUTTER

Yield: 3 cups

Heat Scale: Mild to medium

Fruit butter is a sweet fruit spread for breads, but the process is a bit different from jelly-making because it relies on long cooking times rather than pectin. Lynda Pozel supplied this recipe, noting, "Apple butter has been a favorite since colonial times, and is usually made with cider, fruit, sugar, cinnamon, and other sweet spices. This recipe is further spiced with chile."

$3^{1}/_{2}$ cups apple cider

8 large sweet apples (such as Golden Delicious)

$^{1}/_{3}$ cup stemmed, seeded, and finely chopped fresh chiles (green New Mexican for mildly spiced and jalapeño for more fire)

Sugar to taste

$1^{1}/_{2}$ teaspoons ground cinnamon

Place the cider, apples, and chile in a heavy saucepan bring to a boil, reduce the heat and simmer, uncovered, for 45 minutes.

Add the sugar and cinnamon and continue simmering uncovered until mixture is the consistency of thick applesauce, about 20 to 25 minutes.

Ladle the hot apple butter into half-pint jars, leaving $^{1}/_{4}$ inch at the top. Wipe the rims with a clean cloth and close with jar lids and rings. Let cool. Label and store in cool, dark spot.

DATIL-PINEAPPLE PEAR RELISH

Yield: About twelve 1-pint jars
Heat Scale: Medium to hot

🔥 🔥 🔥

This recipe by Irene Day Randall is from St. Johns County, Florida, and was first published in Chile Pepper *magazine. Irene says the recipe has been around for years. "Pineapple pears" are pears that are hard even when fully ripe. In some produce markets, they are know as "hard green cooking pears." Usually they're available in the fall. Serve this with grilled or roasted meats or seafood. This recipe makes a lot of relish, so give away some of the jars as gifts.*

6 to 8 datil chiles or 3 habaneros, stemmed and seeded

12 pineapple pears, peeled and chopped

6 bell peppers, stemmed, seeded, and chopped

2 onions, chopped

2 cups distilled white vinegar

1 cup loosely packed brown sugar

1 cup white granulated sugar

1 tablespoon salt

2 tablespoons prepared mustard

1 teaspoon celery seed

$^1/_2$ teaspoon turmeric

Place the datil peppers, pears, bell peppers, onions, and vinegar in a food processor, a little at a time, and coarsely chop or grind. Add remaining ingredients and cook slowly, uncovered over medium heat, for $^1/_2$ hour. Put in sterile 1-pint jars and seal.

SWEET GREEN MANGO CHUTNEY
WITH HABANERO

Yield: About 3 cups
Heat Scale: Medium

We collected this recipe during tours of the eastern Caribbean. Because of a heavy influence from East Indian immigrants, chutneys are enormously popular in the region, and the local cooks make them hot with habanero chiles and sweet with brown sugar. Note: This recipe requires advance preparation. It is best used after it has matured for 1 month.

6 green mangoes, peeled, pitted, and diced

2 (3-inch) pieces ginger, peeled

4 cloves garlic, peeled

$^1/_3$ cup distilled white vinegar

$^1/_4$ cup chopped dates

$^3/_4$ cup currants

$^1/_2$ cup raisins

1 habanero chile, stemmed, seeded, and minced

1 teaspoon salt

$^1/_4$ cup firmly packed brown sugar

$^1/_2$ cup distilled white vinegar

In a food processor, combine the mangoes, ginger, garlic, and the $^1/_3$ cup of vinegar, and purée. Transfer to a bowl, cover, and refrigerate overnight.

The next day, combine the dates, currants, raisins, and habanero in a food processor and purée. Transfer the mixture to a large saucepan, add the mango mixture, the remaining ingredients and bring to a boil. Lower the heat and cook, stirring from time to time until the mixture is thick and syrupy, about $2^1/_2$ to 3 hours. Pour into sterilized jars and seal.

CRANBERRY-CHILE CHUTNEY

Yield: 2 pints

Heat Scale: Medium

This great-tasting hot chutney by Marilou Robinson was one of the winners of the Chile Pepper *magazine recipe contest. Serve it with grilled or roasted meats or even with curries. This chutney will keep for several weeks in the refrigerator.*

- 2 cups fresh or frozen cranberries
- 1 large onion, chopped
- 4 cloves garlic, minced
- $^1/_4$ cup cider vinegar
- 3 tablespoons granulatd sugar (or more to taste)
- 1 cup cranberry juice
- 1 tablespoon Tabasco® Pepper Sauce
  (or substitute any Louisiana-style hot sauce)
- 1 tablespoon Lee Kum Kee Chili Paste
  (or substitute any Asian chile paste)
- $^1/_4$ cup chopped red bell pepper
- 1 red jalapeño chile, stemmed, seeded, and chopped
- 1 cup dried cranberries

Place all the ingredients in a saucepan. Bring to a boil, reduce the heat, and simmer for 45 minutes, or until the chutney is thick. Cool and refrigerate.

6

CAPSICUM CAKES

For centuries, cake has been one of the most traditional desserts served on important occasions. From weddings to baptisms and even funerals, cake has helped celebrate the beginnings and endings of life's important moments. That's a lot of performance pressure on one little dish! Fortunately, our cupboard is full of both exciting and extraordinary, as well as elegant and exceptional, cake recipes fit for a king, president or pope, as well as for you and me.

With that note, we introduce cakes that offer new twists on old favorites and fruity temptations, cakes sweet enough to please but just hot enough for a champion of chiles.

There are moist, exceptionally rich, and luscious cakes, and cheesecakes with the combination of chiles and cheese sure to please. We hope our fiery cakes will please and inspire you to create some of your own sizzling selections.

MANDARIN ORANGE-WALNUT
PEQUIN CAKE

Yield: 8 servings

Heat Scale: Hot

This citrus delight is simple to prepare and and just tart enough to complement the sweet-hot glaze. It can be nice made in a 9-inch bundt pan.

2 cups granulated sugar

2 cups flour

2 eggs

2 (4-ounce) cans mandarin oranges, with juices

1 cup walnuts, chopped

2 teaspoons baking soda

$^1/_2$ teaspoon salt

1 teaspoon vanilla extract

GLAZE

1 cup firmly packed brown sugar

6 tablespoons butter

4 tablespoons milk

$^1/_8$ teaspoon salt

$^1/_2$ teaspoon vanilla extract

6 pequin chiles, seeded, stemmed, and ground,
   or 1 teaspoon cayenne

Preheat oven to 350°. Grease a 9 by 13-inch pan.

In a large mixing bowl, combine the granulated sugar, flour, eggs, oranges and juices, walnuts, baking soda, salt, and vanilla. Mix by hand, being careful not to overmix. Pour the batter into the prepared pan and bake for 45 minutes.

Place the brown sugar, butter, milk, salt, vanilla and pequin powder in a saucepan. Stir the mixture and bring it to a boil. Let the glaze cool for about 5 minutes, then drizzle it over the cake.

DOROTHY'S SPICED
RAW APPLE CAKE

Yield: 12 servings
Heat Scale: Medium

🔥 🔥

Melissa's mother-in-law contributed this recipe to which we added a New Mexico flair with the green chile. This cake explodes with flavor from the chile and apples fresh from the harvest.

2 cups granulated sugar

4 cups apples, peeled, cored, and sliced

$^1/_2$ cup green chile, roasted, peeled, stemmed, seeded, and chopped

2 cups all-purpose flour

1 teaspoon salt

$1^1/_2$ teaspoons baking soda

2 teaspoons cinnamon

2 eggs, beaten

$^3/_4$ cup vegetable oil

2 teaspoons vanilla extract

Preheat the oven to 350°. Grease a 9 by 13-inch pan.

In a large mixing bowl, mix the sugar, apples and green chile, then set aside.

In a separate bowl, combine the flour, salt, baking soda, and cinnamon. Add the dry ingredients to the apple mixture, and mix in the eggs, vegetable oil, and vanilla. Mix thoroughly, then pour into the prepared pan. Bake for 50 minutes.

NOT YOUR AUNT BERTHA'S FRUITCAKE

Yield: 12 servings

Heat Scale: Medium

Before you turn the page and go on to another recipe, stop and give this a try. This is not the famed traveling fruitcake recipe—the mythological fruitcake that never spoils and is never eaten. Nope, this is a green chile fruitcake—new, improved, and spunkier than ever.

3 cups chopped pecans (about 12 ounces)

2 cups chopped candied pineappple (about 10 ounces)

3/4 cup chopped dried mangoes

1/3 cup (about 1 1/2 ounces) chopped candied orange zest

1 3/4 cups plus 3 tablespoons all-purpose flour

1 cup butter, softened

1 cup granulated sugar

5 eggs

1/2 cup roasted, peeled, stemmed, seeded, and chopped
   green chiles

1 tablespoon vanilla extract

1 tablespoon lemon extract

1 teaspoon banana extract

1/2 teaspoon baking powder

Pinch of salt

Confectioners' sugar

Position the oven rack in lowest third of oven, and preheat to 250°. Grease and flour a 12-cup bundt pan. In a large bowl, mix the pecans and fruits with 3 tablespoons flour. In another large bowl, cream the butter with the granulated sugar with an electric mixer until light and fluffy. Beat in the eggs 1 at a time. Stir in the green chile, vanilla, lemon, and banana extracts. Sift the 1 3/4 cups flour with the baking powder and salt. Add the dry ingredients to batter, stir until blended, then mix the fruit mixture into batter.

Pour batter into the prepared pan. Bake the cake until it turns golden brown and a toothpick inserted into the center comes out clean, about $2^1/_2$ hours. Cool in the pan on a wire rack for about 15 minutes; turn it out onto the rack and cool. Dust with confectioners' sugar.

BLISTERING BITE-SIZED CHEESECAKES

Yield: 12

Heat Scale: Medium

You'll love these mini-cakes of sorts. Why not offer a variety of toppings such as a selection of fiery fruits from Chapter 8, or a chile-spiked chocolate sauce? Let your guests help themselves!

12 vanilla wafers

2 (8-ounce) packages light cream cheese, softened

$^1/_2$ cup granulated sugar

1 serrano chile, stemmed, seeded, and minced

1 tablespoon vanilla extract

2 eggs

Line two 6-cup muffin tins with foil cupcake liners. Place one vanilla wafer in each liner.

With an electric mixer, combine the cream cheese, vanilla, sugar, and serrano on medium speed until well blended. Add the eggs and mix well. Pour the mixture over the wafers, filling three-quarters full. Bake 25 minutes at 325°.

Remove from pans when cool. Chill before serving.

HAWAII FIVE-O-SO-HOT
UPSIDE-DOWN CAKE

Yield: 8 servings
Heat Scale: Medium

We collected this recipe while on a trip to Maui. If possible, we suggest that you substitute fresh pineapple for the canned. After tasting pinapple taken right off of the plant, you'll discover there's almost nothing better than this fresh tropical treat.

$^1/_4$ cup butter or margarine

$^3/_4$ cup firmly packed light brown sugar

1-pound, 4-ounce can pineapple slices, drained

1 jalapeño chile, stemmed, seeded, and chopped

10 maraschino cherries

10 pecan halves

$1^1/_4$ cups sifted all-purpose flour

$1^3/_4$ teaspoons baking powder

$^1/_2$ teaspoon salt

$^1/_4$ cup shortening

1 cup granulated sugar

1 egg

$^1/_2$ cup plus 1 teaspoon milk

$1^1/_4$ teaspoons vanilla extract

$^1/_4$ teaspoon lemon extract

$^3/_4$ teaspoon grated orange zest

$^3/_4$ teaspoon grated lemon zest

$^1/_2$ cup shredded coconut

Preheat oven to 350°.

Melt the butter in a 9-inch cake pan. Mix in the brown sugar. Arrange the pineapple slices and jalapeño pieces close together in the mixture in a single layer. Cut the remaining slices in halves and stand around sides of the pan. Place a cherry and a pecan halve in the center of each slice. Set aside.

In a large mixing bowl, sift together the flour, baking powder, and salt. Beat the shortening and granulated sugar with an electric mixer until light and fluffy. Beat in the egg. Add the flour mixture alternately with the milk, mixing well. Stir in the vanilla and lemon extracts and the orange and lemon zests; fold in the coconut.

Spread batter over the pineapple in the prepared pan. Bake for 55 to 65 minutes, or until a toothpick inserted in the center of the cake comes out clean.

Remove the cake from the oven and let it stand in the pan for 15 minutes. Run a knife blade around the edge to loosen and carefully invert the cake onto a serving plate.

DRY CAKES NO MORE!

• To make your cakes moist, try adding a teaspoon or two of honey to the batter.

• To salvage an over-baked cake, drizzle a little Kahlúa, Grand Marnier, or Tia Maria over the top.

• The freshest butter makes the freshest cakes. To keep butter fresh, skip storing it in the butter slot in your refrigerator. Instead, store it in its original container in the coldest part of your refrigerator, where it will stay fresh for up to 30 days.

DEVILISH
ANGEL FOOD CAKE

Yield: 12 servings
Heat Scale: Medium

Chocolate angel food cake with a hint of heat describes this delectable cake. Try topping it with with spiced-up confectioners' sugar for a new dining experience.

$^3/_4$ cup sifted cake flour (not self-rising)

1 tablespoon New Mexican red chile powder

$^1/_4$ cup unsweetened cocoa powder

$1^1/_4$ cups egg whites (from about 12 large eggs)

$^1/_4$ teaspoon salt

1 teaspoon cream of tartar

$1^1/_4$ cups sifted granulated sugar

1 teaspoon vanilla extract or lemon juice

TOPPING

$^1/_2$ cup confectioners' sugar

1 teaspoon New Mexican red chile powder

Preheat oven to 375°. Sift together thoroughly flour, red chile powder, and cocoa. Resift the mixture at least 5 times to ensure a light and airy cake. Set aside. In a large chilled bowl, beat the egg whites and salt until they are foamy, then sprinkle with the cream of tartar. Gradually add the granulated sugar and beat until stiff. Fold in the vanilla, and then the flour-cocoa mixture, using an over-and-under motion.

Pour the batter into an ungreased 10-inch tube pan and bake for 30 to 35 minutes, or until a toothpick inserted in the middle of the cake comes out clean. Remove cake from the oven and cool until barely warm; remove from pan. Combine the confectioners' sugar and red chile powder in a sifter, sift over the cake, and serve.

CHOCOLATE-RED CHILE ZUCCHINI CAKE

Yield: 12 servings
Heat Scale: Medium

Red Chile and chocolate is an elegant combination. The zucchini makes this cake extra moist and extra delicious.

$2^1/_2$ cups sifted flour

$^1/_4$ cup unsweetened cocoa

1 teaspoon baking soda

1 teaspoon salt

$^1/_2$ cup butter

$^1/_2$ cup vegetable oil

$1^3/_4$ cups granulated sugar

2 eggs

1 teaspoon vanilla extract

1 tablespoon New Mexican red chile powder

$^1/_2$ cup buttermilk

2 cups grated zucchini

6 ounces semisweet chocolate chips

$^3/_4$ cup chopped walnuts

Preheat oven to 325°. Grease a 9 by 13 by 2-inch pan.

Sift together flour, cocoa, baking soda, and salt in a large mixing bowl. Set aside.

In a separate bowl, cream the butter, vegetable oil, and sugar, beating until the mixture is light and fluffy. Beat in eggs, one at a time. Next, add the vanilla and chile powder. Mix in the dry ingredients, alternating with the buttermilk. Stir in the zucchini.

Pour the batter into the prepared pan. Sprinkle the top of the cake with the chocolate chips and walnuts. Bake for about 55 minutes or until a toothpick inserted in center comes out clean. Cool cake in the pan on a wire rack.

RED HOT CHILE
CARROT CAKE

Yield: 16 servings
Heat Scale: Medium

This recipe is from David Paul's Lahaina Grill in Lahaina, Maui. This dessert may make you sing and is a guaranteed hit at any affair. It's also a really pretty cake, and is especially attractive when you save an assortment of chiles to garnish the platter.

   $^3/_4$ pound butter

   $1^1/_2$ cups granulated sugar

   $1^1/_2$ teaspoons vanilla extract

   4 eggs

   1 egg yolk

   $1^1/_2$ teaspoons baking soda

   1 teaspoon ground cinnamon

   $2^1/_4$ cups all-purpose flour

   2 cups shredded carrots

   10 pequin chiles, seeded, stemmed, and finely ground
      (or 1 teaspooon cayenne powder)

   2 ounces simple sugar syrup

   2 ounces cinnamon schnapps

   $^1/_4$ cup chopped pistachios

FROSTING

   1 cup water

   $2^1/_4$ cups granulated sugar

   1 cup egg whites

   2 pounds unsalted butter, cut into small chunks

   1 pound softened cream cheese, cut into small chunks

Preheat oven to 350°. Grease and flour a round10-inch cake pan.

Whip butter, sugar, and vanilla together until creamy. Add the eggs one at a time, beating until absorbed.

In a separate bowl, sift together flour, baking soda, and cinnamon and gradually add the dry mixture to the wet mixture in 4 parts. Fold in the carrots and the pequins.

Place the batter in the prepared pan and gently tap the pan to remove any air bubbles. Bake for approximately 1 hour. Test the center of the cake with a toothpick; when it comes out clean the cake is done. Place the cake on a wire rack to cool. When cool, cut the cake into three equal layers. Moisten the layers with the syrup and schnapps.

To make the frosting, place the water and sugar in a large saucepan and, using a candy thermometer, heat the mixture to 121°. Let the mixture cool to 95°, then using an electric mixer, whip the egg whites into fluffy peaks. Add the liquid sugar to the egg whites in a slow, steady stream. Add the butter and cream cheese in small chunks. Whip the mixture into a smooth, creamy consistency. Top the first layer with frosting. Place the second cake layer on top of the first and frost the top of it. Add the third cake layer and then frost the top of it and the sides of all 3 cake layers. Finally, coat the outside of the cake with chopped pistachios.

SIMPLE SYRUP

Simple syrup, also called sugar syrup, is a solution of sugar and water that is cooked over low heat until clear, then boiled for a minute. To make simple syrup, combine 2 tablespoons sugar with 3 tablespoons water in a saucepan and stir continuously over low heat until the sugar is dissolved. Next, bring the mixture to a boil. Remove from the heat, cool, and use. Yield: $^1/_4$ cup.

GRAND MARNIER
CAKE WITH A KICK

Yield: 16 servings
Heat Scale: Mild

This three-level-high tower of heat is not only hot and tasty, it's smooth and sweet. You might like to substitute Kahlúa for the Grand Marnier for a nice change.

$3/4$ cup margarine, softened

$2^1/4$ cups granulated sugar

4 eggs

2 ounces unsweetened baking chocolate, melted

$^1/3$ cup Grand Marnier

$2^1/4$ cups sifted cake flour

4 teaspoons green chile powder

1 teaspoon cream of tartar

$^1/2$ teaspoon baking soda

$^1/4$ teaspoon salt

$3/4$ cup milk

CHOCOLATE-GRAND MARNIER FROSTING

$^1/4$ cup butter, softened

1 (8-ounce) package cream cheese, softened

1 (16-ounce) box confectioners' sugar, sifted

3 ounces unsweetened baking chocolate, melted

$^1/4$ cup Grand Marnier

$3/4$ cup chopped hazelnuts

Preheat oven to 350°. Grease and flour 3 round 9-inch cake pans.
Whip the butter at medium speed with an electric mixer, gradually adding the sugar. Add the eggs, one at a time, beating well after each addition. Add the chocolate and Grand Marnier; beat until blended.

In a separate bowl, combine the flour, chile powder, cream of tartar, baking soda, and salt. Add the dry ingredients alternately with the milk to the creamed mixture, beginning and ending with flour mixture. Mix well after each addition.

Pour the batter into the 3 prepared cake pans. Bake 18 to 23 minutes or until a toothpick inserted in the cake center comes out clean. Cool in the pans for 10 minutes. Remove from pans, and cool completely on wire racks.

To make the frosting, in a large bowl beat the butter and cream cheese at medium speed with an electric mixer. Add 1 cup of the confectioners' sugar and the chocolate; beat until smooth. Gradually add the remaining confectioners' sugar and Grand Marnier, beating at a low speed until smooth enough to spread.

Stir $^1/_2$ cup of the hazelnuts into 1 cup of frosting. Top the first cake layer with frosting. Place the second cake layer on top of the first and frost the top of it. Add the third cake layer and then frost the top of it and the sides of all 3 cake layers. Sprinkle the remaining hazelnuts over the top of the frosted cake.

BURN-THE-ROOF-OF-YOUR-MOUTH CAKE

Yield: 16 servings

Heat Scale: Medium

Yes, we know it seems a little lazy to include a recipe that calls for a packaged cake mix. However, you'll thank us when you find out at the last minute that company is coming—this cake looks and tastes like it took hours to make. Only you will know how easy it was!

1 yellow cake mix

$2^{1}/_{2}$ cups creamy peanut butter

$3/_{4}$ cup chocolate syrup

8 ounces semisweet chocolate chips

2 teaspoons cayenne powder

1 cup confectioners' sugar

$^{1}/_{4}$ cup milk

Chopped pine nuts

Preheat oven to 350°. Grease and flour two 9-inch cake pans.

Prepare the cake according to the package directions, beating $^{1}/_{2}$ cup of the peanut butter into the well-mixed batter.

Divide the batter between the cake pans. Bake for 20 minutes, or until a toothpick inserted into the center of each comes out clean. Cool the cake layers in their pans on cooling racks for 10 minutes. Turn the cakes out onto the racks and cool competely.

In a small saucepan, combine the chocolate syrup and semisweet chocolate. Stir constantly over low heat until the chocolate is melted and the mixture is smooth; transfer mixture to a large bowl. Stir in the remaining 2 cups peanut butter, then the cayenne powder, confectioners' sugar, and the milk. Continue stirring until smooth. Place 1 cake layer on a platter. Spread $1^{1}/_{2}$ cups icing over the top of the first cake layer. Top with the second cake layer. Spread the top of the second layer and sides of both layers with the remaining icing. Garnish with chopped pine nuts.

NO-COOK PEANUT AND
CHILE CHEESECAKE

Yield: 10 servings
Heat Scale: Medium

This may be the easiest dessert you'll ever make. You can whip it up fast when the hankering for a bit of heat hits you. Be sure to cut this cake into little slices unless you or your guests are nuts about peanut butter. This is so rich tasting, a little goes a long way.

1 cup crunchy peanut butter

2 (8-ounce) packages cream cheese

2 dried Thai chiles, seeded, stemmed, and ground,
   or $^{1}/_{2}$ teaspoon cayenne powder

1$^{3}/_{4}$ cup confectioners' sugar

1 (12-ounce) container of frozen whipped topping

1 prepared chocolate crust

2 cups semisweet chocolate chips

In a large bowl, mix the peanut butter, cream cheese, chiles, confectioners' sugar, and frozen whipped topping together. Blend well. Pour the mixture into the prepared pie shell, smooth until level with a plastic spatula, and refrigerate. Garnish with chocolate chips and serve.

PUNGENT PRALINE PUMPKIN CHEESECAKE

Yield: 16 servings
Heat Scale: Medium

You'll go nuts over this hot nutty cheesecake. We've rocked and rolled these ever-so-wonderful macadamia nuts in New Mexico red chile powder to create pralines like you've never had before. Note: This recipe requires advance preparation.

CRUST

$1^1/_2$ cups finely ground gingersnap cookies

$3/_4$ cup ground macadamia nuts

3 tablespoons firmly packed brown sugar

1 tablespoon New Mexican red chile powder

6 tablespoons unsalted butter, melted and cooled

FILLING

$1^1/_2$ pounds cream cheese, at room temperature

1 cup firmly packed brown sugar

$1^1/_2$ cups canned solid pack pumpkin

$1/_2$ cup whipping cream

$1/_3$ cup pure maple syrup

1 tablespoon vanilla extract

$3/_4$ teaspoon ground cinnamon

$1/_8$ teaspoon ground allspice

$1/_8$ teaspoon ground ginger

4 large eggs

PRALINES

2 tablespoons butter

$1^1/_4$ cups granulated sugar

6 tablespoons water

2 teaspoons New Mexican red chile powder

1 cup coarsely chopped toasted macadamia nuts

Preheat oven to 325°.

Mix the gingersnaps, macadamia nuts, brown sugar, and red chile in a medium bowl. Add the butter and stir until well combined. Press the crumb mixture onto the bottom and 2 inches up sides of a 9-inch spring-form pan with $2^3/_4$-inch-high sides. Bake for 8 minutes, then set aside to cool.

Using an electric mixer, beat the cream cheese and brown sugar in bowl until fluffy. Beat in pumpkin. Add the whipping cream, maple syrup, vanilla, cinnamon, allspice, and ginger and mix until smooth. Add the eggs 1 at a time, beating just until combined. Pour batter into the prepared crust and bake for about $1^1/_2$ hours until the cheesecake is puffed and center is set (cheesecake will rise slightly above edge of pan). Transfer the cake to a rack and cool for 30 minutes. Run a small sharp knife around the edge of the cheesecake to loosen. Cool completely. Cover and refrigerate overnight. (Can be prepared 2 days ahead.)

To make the pralines, line a baking sheet with foil. Butter the foil. Combine the sugar and water in a heavy saucepan over low heat, stirring until the sugar dissolves. Increase the heat and boil without stirring, until syrup turns deep golden brown. Brush down the sides of the pan with a pastry brush dipped in water and occasionally swirl the syrup. Stir in the red chile powder and macadamia nuts. Immediately pour the praline mixture onto the prepared baking sheet, spreading with the back of a spoon to a thickness of about $^1/_4$ inch. Cool completely. Break the praline into 2-inch jagged pieces, then place the pieces in a food processor and grind into a chunky powder. (Can be prepared 1 day ahead. Refrigerate in airtight container.)

Transfer the cheesecake to a platter and release the pan sides. Arrange the praline mixture atop the cheesecake. Cut the cheesecake into wedges and serve.

SPICY JAM CAKES

Yield: 24

Heat Scale: Medium

The heat is in the jam on this attractive dessert, and this cake gives you a great excuse to make up a batch of Pineapple-Datil Jelly (page 84).

$^3/_4$ cup well-chilled unsalted butter, cut into 12 pieces

$^1/_4$ cup granulated sugar

1 tablespoon sour cream

1 teaspoon vanilla extract

$^1/_4$ teaspoon salt

$1^1/_2$ cups unbleached all-purpose flour

$^1/_4$ cup Pineapple-Datil Jelly (page 84)

2 tablespoons confectioners' sugar

Position the rack in the center of the oven and preheat to 350°.

In a food processor, chop the butter with the sugar until the butter is the size of small peas, pulsing 4 to 5 times. Add the sour cream, vanilla, and salt and blend just until combined, pulsing about 10 times. Sprinkle the flour over the mixture, and blend just until even grainlike crumbs form, about 15 seconds.

Press 1 generous teaspoon of crumb mixture into 24 miniature muffin cups. Bake until the edges of each cake are just golden, about 22 minutes.

When you remove the cakes from the oven, immediately make a $^3/_8$-inch-deep indentation into the center of each cake using the end of a wooden spoon. Fill each with about $^1/_2$ teaspoon of the preserves. Let the cakes cool in the pan for about 10 minutes. Transfer them to wire racks and cool competely. Just before serving, sprinkle confectioners' sugar over the top of each cake.

BUTTER CAKE WITH TANGERINES, CINNAMON, CAYENNE, AND CHOCOLATE

Yield: 8 servings

Heat Scale: Mild

Although the name may make you think this recipe is a bit complicated at first glance from the recipe title, this adaptation of a Dutch treat is actually fairly simple to make, and definitely good to the last bite.

$3/_4$ cup plus 2 tablespoons superfine sugar

2 tablespoons beaten egg

Grated zest of 1 large lemon

$^1/_4$ teaspoon salt

$1^1/_2$ cups plus 2 tablespoons unsalted butter, softened

$2^1/_4$ cups all-purpose flour

2 tablespoons water

Tangerines with Cinammon, Cayenne, and
   Chocolate (page 151)

In a large bowl, mix the sugar with the egg and lemon zest. Place mixture in a food processor, add the salt and softened butter, and process, pulsing until the mixture resembles a coarse meal. Add the flour a little at a time to the mixture, processing until you have a dough ball.

Pat the dough in a 9-inch round cake pan, cover, and refrigerate for 3 hours.

Preheat oven to 375° and bake the cake uncovered in the middle of the oven for 15 to 17 minutes. (It will seem very soft.) Remove and let cool until it is firm. Slice and serve topped with the Tangerines, Cinnamon, Cayenne, and Chocolate.

7

PIE PANDEMONIUM &
TORRID TARTS

Who would have guessed that something as simple as a pie would have inspired this book? In 1994, Melissa brought one of the winning desserts of that year's *Chile Pepper* recipe contest to Thanksgiving dinner at the DeWitts'. The dessert? It was Hot Chocolate Pecan Pie, featuring Chimayó red chile from New Mexico.

At the dinner was noted Albuquerque morning personality T.J. Trout, who had been promoting his weight-loss and no-fat diet on the air for months. T.J. was persuaded to try a half-inch slice of pie. He tasted, nodded his head, and then requested another piece.

Three slices of pie later, a diet was destroyed, and a cookbook idea was born. With that we introduce a scorching selection of pies and tarts to surprise and delight you.

GERMAN CHOCOLATE-PINE NUT PIE

Yield: 8 servings

Heat Scale: Medium

It's hard to beat the combination of chocolate, nuts, and coconut. Add some jalapeño powder and you've got a powerfully wonderful dessert. We use a prepared crust in this recipe, but feel free to borrow any of the other crust recipes in the book if you feel like making your own.

4 ounces sweet baking chocolate

$^1/_4$ cup margarine

1 (14-ounce) can light sweetened condensed milk

2 eggs, slightly beaten

$^1/_2$ cup hot water

1 teaspoon vanilla extract

2 teaspoons jalapeño powder

$^1/_8$ teaspoon salt

1 prepared unbaked 9-inch pie shell

$^1/_2$ cup chopped pine nuts

1 cup flaked unsweetened coconut

1 jalapeño, stemmed, seeded, and cut into rings (optional)

Whipped cream topping

Preheat oven to 350°.

In a heavy saucepan, melt the chocolate and margarine over low heat. When the chocolate is melted, remove from the heat and set aside. In a large mixing bowl, combine the chocolate mixture and the condensed milk. Next stir in the eggs, hot water, vanilla, jalapeño powder, and salt. Mix well until all of the ingredients are combined. Pour the mixture into the prepared crust, and top with the pine nuts and coconut. Bake 35 to 45 minutes, or until the coconut is lightly browned. Garnish with the jalapeño rings and whipped cream.

TART APPLE PIE

Yield: 8 servings
Heat Scale: Medium

There are easier apple pie recipes, however, we promise you'll think this fruity hot pie is worth the trouble.

CRUST

$2^1/_2$ cups all-purpose flour

1 teaspoon salt

1 teaspoon granulated sugar

$^1/_2$ cup chilled unsalted butter, cut into pieces

$^1/_2$ cup chilled solid vegetable shortening

$1^1/_2$ teaspoons cider vinegar

4 to 5 tablespoons ice water

FILLING

$2^2/_3$ cups apple cider

8 Granny Smith apples, peeled, cored, and sliced

2 Golden Delicious apples, peeled, cored, and sliced

$^1/_2$ cup green chiles, roasted, peeled, stemmed, seeded, and chopped

1 cup granulated sugar

$^1/_4$ cup all-purpose flour

$^1/_2$ teaspoon ground cinnamon

$^1/_4$ teaspoon ground mace

$^1/_4$ teaspoon salt

4 teaspoons fresh lemon juice

3 tablespoons unsalted butter, cut into small pieces

To make the crust, combine the flour, salt, and sugar in a food processor. Add the butter and shortening and process until the mixture resembles a coarse meal. Combine the vinegar and 2 tablespoons of the ice water in a small bowl. Add to flour mixture. With the food processor running, gradually add enough remaining water, 1 tablespoon at a time to form moist clumps of dough. Next, gather the dough into 2 balls. Flatten into disks. Wrap each disk in plastic. Chill for 30 minutes.

To make the filling, boil the cider in a heavy saucepan until reduced to $^2/_3$ cup, about 25 minutes. Cool.

Position the oven rack in the lowest third of oven and preheat to 425°.

In a large mixing bowl, combine the apples, chiles, sugar, flour, cinnamon, mace, and salt. Add the reduced cider and the lemon juice and toss well. Set aside.

Roll out 1 pie crust on a lightly floured surface to a round 14-inches in diameter. Roll up dough on rolling pin and transfer to a 10-inch pie plate. Gently press the crust into place. Trim the edges of crust, leaving a $^1/_2$-inch overhang. Spoon the apple mixture into the crust, mounding the apples in the center. Dot the apples with the butter.

Roll out the second crust on a lightly floured surface to a round 13 inches in diameter. Roll the dough up on the rolling pin and unroll over the apples. Trim edges, leaving $^3/_4$-inch overhang. Fold overhang of the top crust under the edge of the bottom crust. Pinch together the edges of the upper and bottom crusts to seal. Crimp edges. Cut several slashes in the top crust to allow steam to escape. Cover the edges with foil so that they do not brown too quickly.

Bake the pie for 25 minutes. Reduce the oven temperature to 350°. Continue baking until the filling bubbles, about 50 minutes longer. Cool. Serve pie slightly warm.

WHO NEEDS SEX WHEN THERE'S APPLE PIE?

"A lot of people have never really had the chance to eat a decent apple pie, but after a minute's sensual reflection will know positively what to expect if they did. They can taste it on their mind's tongue: Thick flaky pastry; and hunks of sweet apple bathed in syrup, rich but sturdy dough filled with finely sliced apple tarts seasoned with cinnamon; an upper and lower crust in a traditional pie pan; an upper crust only, in a deep dish; a bottom crust with crosses of dough over the filling."

—M.F.K. Fisher

PUMPKIN PIE WITH A
KISS OF CAYENNE

Yield: 6 servings

Heat Scale: Medium

Many people are flabbergasted when they read a recipe that contains lard. Contrary to popular belief, using a little lard will not seriously harm you. We believe that for a truly flaky pie crust, lard almost has to be in the ingredient list.

CRUST

$^1/_2$ cup unsalted butter, cut into bits

3 tablespoons lard, cut into bits

$1^3/_4$ cups flour

$^1/_4$ teaspoon salt

$^1/_2$ teaspoon granulated sugar

$^1/_3$ cup cold water

FILLING

2 eggs

1 cup canned solid pack pumpkin

$^1/_2$ cup firmly packed light brown sugar

$^1/_2$ teaspoon ground allspice

$^1/_2$ teaspoon ground cinnamon

$^1/_4$ teaspoon ground ginger

2 teaspoons cayenne powder

$^1/_4$ teaspoon salt

$^3/_4$ cup light cream

TOPPING

1 cup coarsely chopped pecans

2 tablespoons melted butter

1 teaspoon cayenne powder

$^{1}/_{4}$ cup loosely packed light brown sugar

1 cup heavy cream, chilled

1 teaspoon granulated sugar

1 tablespoon vanilla extract

Lightly butter a 9-inch pie plate.

In a deep bowl, cut the butter and lard pieces into the flour with a knife and fork or pastry blender until the mixture resembles a coarse meal. In a small bowl, dissolve the salt and sugar in the cold water. Stir the liquids into the flour to form a loose ball of dough.

Knead the chunks of dough on a lightly floured surface, distributing the butter and lard through the mixture with the heel of your hand. Reshape the dough into a ball, dust lightly with flour and chill for 30 minutes.

Roll out the chilled dough on a lightly floured surface until it is a rough square $^{1}/_{4}$ inch thick with 12-inch-long sides. Fold the square in half diagonally once and then twice, like a handkerchief, until it is one quarter the size of the original square. Place the dough in the center of the preapred pie plate. Unfold the dough, gently easing it into the bottom and along the sides of the plate.

Trim off the dough hanging over the edge of the pie plate, leaving a $^{1}/_{2}$-inch overlap. Fold this overlap back over the edge of the plate and pinch all around to make a decorative edge. Prick the bottom and sides of the dough with a fork, and refrigerate until the filling is completed.

Preheat oven to 400°.

Beat the eggs with an electric mixer until they are frothy in a bowl. Add the pumpkin and brown sugar, stirring well. Add the spices and salt. Stir in the cream, blending thoroughly.

Pour the filling into the pie shell. Place a sheet pan under the oven rack to catch drips. Bake the pie for 45 to 50 minutes. Let cool to set the filling.

Toss the pecans, butter, cayenne powder, and brown sugar together in a small mixing bowl. Spread this mixture evenly over the top.

Whip the cream until peaks form. Stir in the sugar and vanilla. Place the pie under the broiler approximately 4 inches from the heat and broil for about 2 minutes, or until the top is bubbly. Do not let crust brown too quickly. Top with the whipped cream and serve.

PEACHY KEEN
RASPBERRY PIE

Yield: 8 servings

Heat Scale: Hot

$\Diamond$ $\Diamond$ $\Diamond$

Fresh raspberries mix so well with peaches and anchos to create this delicious dessert. Be sure to use fresh fruit.

CRUST

> 3 cups all-purpose flour
>
> $1^1/_2$ teaspoons salt
>
> $^1/_2$ cup vegetable oil
>
> 6 tablespoons skim milk
>
> Vegetable cooking spray

FILLING

> $^1/_3$ cup granulated sugar
>
> 3 tablespoons cornstarch
>
> $^1/_4$ teaspoon ground cinnamon
>
> $^1/_4$ teaspoon ground nutmeg
>
> 3 cups peeled, sliced fresh peaches (about $1^1/_2$ pounds)
>
> 2 teaspoons ancho chile powder
>
> 1 teaspoon lemon juice
>
> $^1/_8$ teaspoon almond extract
>
> 2 cups fresh raspberries

To make the crust, combine the flour and salt in a bowl; add the oil and milk, tossing with a fork until the mixture resembles coarse meal. Gently shape the flour mixture into 2 balls the same size, then cover each with plastic wrap. Place the dough in the refrigerator and chill for 15 minutes.

Roll out each ball of dough, *still covered with the plastic*, into a 12-inch circle; let rest. Remove the plastic wrap covering the second ball of dough. Pat ball into a 9-inch pie plate coated with cooking spray. Trim the edges, reserving trimmings. Gently press a fork around edge of pie plate. Prick the bottom and sides of unbaked crust with a fork, then set aside.

Roll the reserved dough scraps to $^{1}/_{8}$ inch thickness; cut into decorative shapes (we make chile peppers), and set aside. Preheat oven to 425°.

To make the filling, combine the sugar, cornstarch, cinnamon, and nutmeg in a bowl; stir well and set aside. Cut the peach slices in half. Combine the peaches, ancho powder, lemon juice, almond extract, and 3 tablespoons of the sugar mixture in a large bowl; toss gently. In a separate bowl, combine the raspberries and remaining sugar mixture; toss gently. Place the raspberry mixture in the pie shell, then top with peach mixture. Place the reserved pie crust on top of the pie. Pinch together the edges of the upper and bottom crusts to seal. Cut vents in the top of the pie, then arrange the decorative dough shapes on top of the crust. Bake 40 minutes or until bubbly. Cool on a wire rack.

Note: To prevent the crust from burning, cover the edges with aluminum foil during the last 10 minutes of baking.

WHEN "FLAKY" IS A COMPLIMENT

A teaspoon of vinegar added to pie dough will guarantee a flaky crust.

SECRET HABANERO
LEMON MERINGUE PIE

Yield: 8 servings
Heat Scale: Hot

🔥 🔥 🔥

The fruity heat of the habanero combined with the lemon forms the perfect tart and hot taste explosion. We call this our "secret" pie recipe because it can be made very quickly, but tastes like it took all day.

FILLING

4 tablespoons cornstarch

4 tablespoons flour

$^1/_4$ teaspoon salt

$1^1/_4$ cups granulated sugar

$1^1/_2$ cups water

Grated zest of 1 lemon

$^1/_4$ teaspoon habanero powder, or $^1/_4$ stemmed, seeded, and minced fresh habanero

2 tablespoons butter

4 egg yolks, slightly beaten

___

1 prepared graham cracker pie crust

MERINGUE

5 egg whites, at room temperature

$^1/_2$ cup granulated sugar

$^1/_4$ teaspoon salt

Preheat the oven to 425°.

To make the filling, mix the cornstarch, flour, salt, sugar, and water in a saucepan. Cook over medium-high heat, stirring constantly, until thickened, about 2 to 3 minutes. Remove the pan from the heat and stir in the lemon zest, habanero powder, and butter. Slowly add $^1/_2$ cup of the hot mixture into the egg yolks, stirring constantly, then stir the yolks into the remaining hot mixture. Return saucepan to the heat and cook, stirring constantly for 3 more minutes. Remove the lemon mixture from the heat and let cool for a few minutes. Spread the pie filling in the crust, and set aside.

To make the meringue, place the egg whites and sugar in a mixing bowl and set the bowl in a pan of hot water. Stir constantly until the eggs feel warm, then add the salt. Remove the bowl from the hot water, and beat the egg white mixture with an electric beater until the eggs are stiff and shiny. Spread the meringue over the filled pie shell, making sure the meringue touches the inner shell of the crust. Place the pie under the broiler for 1 or 2 minutes or until lightly browned. Remove and serve.

THE HUMBLE BEGINNINGS OF PIE

"Pie is a Middle English word, short for magpie, a reference to the nest of this thieving bird, filled with all sorts of different scavanged material. Early pies were filled with fruits, vegetables, or whatever meat was at hand, and reminded the cooks of a magpie nest."
—The Secret Life of Food

HOT CHOCOLATE PECAN PIE

Yield: 8 to 10 servings
Heat Scale: Medium

This recipe by Stella Fong, of Pavoy, California, was featured on the cover of Chile Pepper when it was selected as a winner in the magazine's 1994 recipe contest. We have added additional heat to the crust to make it a little more pungent.

CHOCOLATE PIE PASTRY

1 cup unbleached all-purpose flour

2 tablespoons unsweetened cocoa

2 tablespoons granulated sugar

3 tablespoons New Mexican red chile powder

$^1/_2$ cup vegetable shortening

$^1/_4$ cup unsalted butter, cut into chunks

2 tablespoons sugar

3 tablespoons cold water

PIE FILLING

4 tablespoons butter

$^1/_4$ cup commercial fudge sauce

3 eggs, beaten

$^3/_4$ cup dark corn syrup

$^1/_2$ cup firmly packed dark brown sugar

2 teaspoons New Mexican red chile powder

1 teaspoon vanilla extract

$1^1/_4$ cups pecan halves

Sift all the dry ingredients together into a food processor. Add the shortening and butter to the food processor, and process until the mixture resembles tiny crumbs, about 1 minute. Add the water and continue to mix until the dough forms a ball.

Wrap the dough in plastic and refrigerate for at least 30 minutes.

Preheat oven to 425°. Line a 9-inch pie pan with the chocolate pie pastry and set aside.

In a microwave-safe bowl, combine the butter and hot fudge and microwave on high for about 1 minute and set aside.

In a large mixing bowl, combine the eggs, corn syrup, sugar, chile powder, fudge mixture, and vanilla. Stir in the pecans and pour the mixture into the pie shell.

Bake the pie for 15 minutes, then reduce the heat to 350°; continue baking for an additional 30 minutes, or until the edges are set.

DANGEROUS DAIQUIRI PIE

Yield: 8 servings
Heat Scale: Medium

This pie is also wonderful when made with frozen lemonade and a shot of tequila. Bottoms up!

8 ounces light cream cheese, softened
1 (14-ounce) can light sweetened condensed milk
2 teaspoons New Mexican red chile powder
1 (6-ounce) can frozen limeade concentrate
$^1/_3$ cup light rum
1 cup frozen whipped topping
1 (9-inch) prepared baked pie shell
Lime slices, cut from edge to center and twisted open

Place cream cheese in a medium-sized mixing bowl and beat with an electric mixer until it is fluffy. Add the condensed milk, red chile powder, and limeade, mixing until smooth. Next, mix in the rum and fold in the frozen whipped topping.

Pour the pie filling into the crust, cover, and chill for at least 2 hours. Garnish with the lime twists and serve.

CHERRANO TURNOVERS

Yield: 6

Heat Scale: Medium

We've combined cherries and serranos to create cherrano turnovers. These personal pies are great to bring along on picnics or eat with some of the hot fruity sorbets in Chapter 10. This is also one of our lowfat recipes. You can find the phyllo dough in the frozen foods section of your grocery store.

Butter-flavored low-calorie cooking spray

1 (16-ounce) can sour pitted cherries, undrained

2 tablespoons cornstarch

$^1/_4$ cup frozen apple juice concentrate

2 serrano chiles or jalapeños, stemmed, seeded, and minced

2 tablespoons granulated sugar

1 teaspoon vanilla extract

6 sheets phyllo dough, thawed and covered with a damp kitchen towel

$^3/_4$ teaspoon ground nutmeg

Preheat oven to 400°. Spray a baking sheet with the cooking spray.

In a small saucepan, combine the cherries, cornstarch, apple juice concentrate, and $1^1/_2$ tablespoons of the sugar. Stir continually until the cornstarch is dissolved. Bring the mixture to a boil, stirring constantly for 1 minute. Remove pan from heat and add the vanilla; let the mixture cool for 10 minutes.

Working with 1 phyllo sheet at a time (keep the others covered with the damp cloth) spray the sheet with the cooking spray. Starting with the long side, fold the phyllo sheet in half, then coat again with the spray. Spoon $^1/_3$ cup of the cherry mixture near one end. Fold the edges inward and carefully roll up, making about a 3 by 4-inch turnover. Place the turnover on the baking sheet and repeat the process until all 6 are assembled.

(continued on page 123)

Pungent Praline
Pumpkin Cheesecake

Habanero Lemon Meringue Pie

In a separate bowl, combine the remaining $1^1/_2$ tablespoons sugar and the nutmeg. Spray the tops of turnovers with the cooking spray, then sprinkle the sugar mixture evenly over each one. Bake for 20 minutes. Cool on a wire rack.

MELTDOWN MINT PIE

Yield: 16 servings
Heat Scale: Hot ◊ ◊ ◊

We use just enough fresh habaneros in this pie to cause a meltdown of sorts; but don't worry—the coolness of the mint and the fact that this pie is served frozen will help put out any fires. Please note that this recipe makes two pies, so why not invite over other chileheads or have a party? Remember to tell your guests that the habanero rings are just for decoration, and should be consumed at their own risk! Note: This recipe requires advance preparation and can be cut in half, if desired.

1 (14-ounce) can light sweetened condensed milk
$^1/_3$ cup crème de menthe
$^1/_4$ cup crème de cacao
$^1/_2$ habanero chile, stemmed, seeded, and minced
2 cups frozen whipped topping
2 (8-inch) prepared chocolate cookie crumb crusts
$^1/_2$ habanero chile, cut into thin rings

In a large bowl, combine the condensed milk, and créme de menthe, créme de cacao, and habanero. Fold whipped topping into the mixture. Pour the filling into the prepared pie crusts. Cover the pies with foil, and freeze for at least 6 hours.

Right before you are ready to serve, garnish the pies with the habanero rings.

BLAZING BANANA
CHERRY TARTLETS

Yield: 16

Heat Scale: Mild

These personal pies are tart and wonderful. They look great, and taste heavenly.

1 sheet (about $^1/_2$ pound) frozen puff pastry, thawed

1 banana, cut diagonally into $^1/_4$-inch-thick slices

1 (8-ounce) can pitted light cherries

$^1/_4$ cup New Mexican green chile, roasted, peeled, stemmed, seeded, and chopped

$1^1/_2$ tablespoons granulated sugar

$^1/_4$ teaspoon ground cinnamon

$1^1/_2$ tablespoons cold unsalted butter, cut into bits

3 tablespoons orange marmalade or a spicy marmalade from Chapter 5

1 teaspoon water

Preheat oven to 400°.

Roll out the pastry $^1/_8$ inch thick on a lightly floured surface. Next cut out two 6-inch rounds, and transfer them to a baking sheet. Arrange the banana slices in the center of the rounds, arranging the cherries around the bananas in a circular pattern completely covering the pastry. Sprinkle the green chile evenly over the bananas and cherries.

In a small bowl, stir together sugar and cinnamon. Sprinkle the mixture over the fruit, dot with the butter, and bake tartlets in the middle of the oven for 25 to 30 minutes, or until the pastry is golden brown.

While the tartlets are baking, place marmalade in a small saucepan and bring it to a boil with the water, stirring constantly. Strain it through a fine sieve into a small bowl. Transfer the tartlets to a rack, brush with the strained marmalade, and let cool until warm.

UNLIKELY LINZER TART

Yield: 8 servings

Heat Scale: Hot

🔥 🔥 🔥

Dan and Melissa first tasted linzer tarts on their honeymoon; the only thing missing was a bit of heat, which is added here.

1 cup all-purpose flour

$^1/_2$ teaspoon baking powder

$^1/_4$ teaspoon ground cinnamon

$^1/_8$ teaspoon ground cloves

$^1/_2$ teaspoon habanero powder

1 teaspoon salt

$1^1/_2$ cups finely ground walnuts

$^3/_4$ cup unsalted butter, at room temperature

$^1/_2$ cup granulated sugar

2 large egg yolks

1 cup raspberry preserves or spicy preserves from Chapter 5

Confectioners' sugar

Preheat the oven to 350°. Butter a 10-inch springform pan.

Sift the flour, baking powder, cinnamon, cloves, and habanero powder into a medium bowl. Stir in the salt and walnuts.

Using an electric mixer, cream the butter and granulated sugar in a large bowl until smooth. Beat in the egg yolks. Add the flour-nut mixture to the butter mixture and mix until blended. Spread $1^3/_4$ cups of the batter on the bottom of the prepared pan. Top with preserves, leaving a $^1/_2$-inch border around the edge. Spoon remaining batter into a pastry bag fitted with a $^3/_8$-inch plain tip. Pipe the batter in a lattice design over preserves. Refrigerate for 20 minutes.

Bake the tart for about 40 minutes, or until the preserves just begin to bubble. Transfer the tart to a wire rack and cool. Just before serving, dust lightly with confectioners' sugar.

SERRANO-LIME TART

Yield: 8 servings
Heat Scale: Medium

This tropical tart of sorts is full of limes and pineapple juice and is sure to sweeten and heat up things a bit. Note: This recipe requires advance preparation.

CRUST

$1^1/_4$ cups unbleached all-purpose flour

2 tablespoons granulated sugar

$^1/_4$ teaspoon salt

$^1/_2$ cup unsalted butter, cut into pieces

1 egg yolk

1 tablespoon cold water

FILLING

$^1/_2$ cup whipping cream

2 tablespoons cornstarch

2 large eggs

6 large egg yolks

$^3/_4$ cup granulated sugar

2 serrano chiles or jalapeños, stemmed, seeded, and minced

$^3/_4$ freshly squeezed lime juice

$^1/_2$ cup pineapple juice

$^1/_2$ cup unsalted butter

Lime zest strips rolled in sugar

To make the crust, place the flour, sugar, and salt in a food processor. Add the butter and cut in pulsing until mixture resembles a coarse meal. Add the egg yolk and water and blend until dough clumps together.

Gather dough into a ball, then flatten. Wrap dough in plastic and refrigerate for 30 minutes.

Roll out the dough on a lightly floured surface to a 13-inch round. Roll up the dough onto the rolling pin and transfer to a 9-inch tart pan with a removable bottom. Press the dough into the pan and trim the edges. Freeze until firm, about 1 hour.

Preheat oven to 400°. Line crust with foil, then fill with dried beans or pie weights. Bake until the rim of the crust is set, about 12 minutes; remove the beans and foil from the crust. Continue baking until the crust is golden in the center, about 14 minutes. Transfer to a wire rack and cool.

To make the filling, place the cream in a bowl. Whisk in the cornstarch. Whisk in the whole eggs and yolks. Combine the sugar, serranos, lime juice, pineapple juice, and butter in a medium saucepan over medium heat. Stir the mixture until the sugar dissolves and the butter melts. Bring to a boil for 1 minute, whisking constantly. Strain into a bowl and cool slightly.

Spoon the filling into tart shell. Chill overnight, and garnish with lime zest strips.

APPLE-PEAR PEPPER TART

Yield: 6 servings

Heat Scale: Medium

This recipe was created specifically to incorporate the Red Jalapeño-Apricot Jelly (page 79)—it's that good! This recipe is a nice morning wakeup call and a perfect partner for a cup of coffee. You may substitute your favorite commercial pepper jelly if you don't have time to make this one.

CRUST

$3/_4$ cup vegetable shortening

$1/_4$ cup boiling water

1 teaspoon salt

1 tablespoon milk

About 2 cups sifted all-purpose flour

FILLING

2 Bartlett pears, peeled, cored, and thinly sliced

1 Granny Smith apple, peeled, cored, and thinly sliced

3 teaspoons lime juice

3 tablespoons granulated sugar

1 tablespoon cornstarch

$1/_4$ teaspoon grated nutmeg

$1/_8$ teaspoon finely ground black pepper

$1/_2$ cup Red Jalapeño–Apricot Jelly (page 79), heated and strained

Frozen whipped topping

Preheat oven to 350°.

To make the crust, place shortening in a large bowl and pour the boiling water over it. Add the salt and milk, blending well. Add $1^{1}/_{2}$ cups of the flour, $^{1}/_{2}$ cup at a time, mixing well after each addition. Add more flour until the mixture clings together and makes a stiff dough. Pat dough into a flat circle, then wrap the dough in plastic, and refrigerate for at least 1 hour.

Roll out the dough on a lightly floured surface. Press the dough into a 10-inch tart pan with a removable bottom. Trim the excess dough. Arrange the pear and apple slices on the dough. Sprinkle the fruit with the lime juice, and set aside. In a separate bowl, combine the sugar, cornstarch, nutmeg, and pepper; sift over the fruit.

Bake for 50 minutes, or until the fruit is tender. While still hot, remove the rim of the pan and slide the tart onto a serving platter. Spread Red Jalapeño–Apricot Jelly over the fruit, cut and serve with a dollop of whipped topping on each piece.

NUCLEAR MACAROON
KIWI TART

Yield: 12 servings

Heat Scale: Hot

This recipe is hot but tasty. The Nuclear Macaroon dough (page 31) makes an interesting base for this awesome kiwifruit tart. However, be sure to double the cookie recipe so you'll have enough dough to make a tart crust.

2 batches of the Nuclear Macaroon Cookie dough (page 31)

$3/4$ cups granulated sugar

3 tablespoons brandy

1 tablespoon lemon juice

Pinch of ground cloves

12 kiwifruit, peeled and cut into $1/4$-inch rounds

Press prepared cookie dough into a tart pan with a removable bottom. Bake at 350° for 13 minutes, checking to make sure it does not burn. When the crust is light brown, remove from the oven and let cool. Remove the sides of the tart pan, place the shell on a serving platter, and set aside.

In a large saucepan, combine the sugar, brandy, lemon juice, and cloves. Stir over high heat until the mixture begins to bubble; boil until it is very thick, for about 13 minutes. Cool the mixture, then pour it over the tart. Place the kiwifruit on the tart in a circular pattern.

THE EASY WAY TO REMOVE TARTS FROM PANS

To remove the sides of a slip-bottom tart tin, place the tart on a tall can and pull the sides downward.

—Conventional Kitchen Wisdom

8

FIERY FRUITS & SPIKED SAUCES

Chiles and fruits are perfectly complementary—perhaps because chiles actually are fruits. Some chiles, particularly habaneros, have fruity aromas and flavors. In exploring the combination of fruits and chiles, we covered as many of each as we could, but the subject seems inexhaustible. An entire book on chiles and fruits will probably be written some day—perhaps even by us! We have also included three hot fruit sauces, for serving over everything from ice cream to barbecue.

GREAT MOMENTS IN THE HISTORY OF CITRUS

310 BC. Theophrastus becomes the first European to mention citrus when he writes of the citron as the Persian apple.

1150. The Arabs introduce the sour orange, pumello, and lemon into Spain.

1565. Citrus first planted in Florida at St. Augustine.

1707. Father Eusebio Kino plants the first citrus in Arizona.

1769. Father Junipero Serra plants the first citrus at Mission San Diego in California.

1841. The first commercial orange grove is planted in California.

1892. Queen Victoria tastes the first California orange imported into England.

1948. Frozen orange juice is available in the United States.

CHILLED CHILE FRUIT SOUP

Yield: 4 servings

Heat Scale: Medium

A quick trip to your local fruit market will determine what fruits will be perfect for this soup. Don't forget peaches!

$^1/_2$ habanero chile, stemmed and seeded

2 cups water

$^1/_4$ cup granulated sugar

1 teaspoon minced fresh ginger

$^1/_2$ teaspoon vanilla extract

Zest of 1 lime

Zest of 1 orange

2 tablespoons minced spearmint leaves

$^1/_4$ cup diced pineapple

$^1/_4$ cup diced mango

$^1/_4$ cup diced papaya

$^1/_4$ cup diced peach

$^1/_4$ cup diced cantaloupe

$^1/_4$ cup diced banana

$^1/_4$ cup chopped orange

$^1/_4$ cup halved strawberries

$^1/_4$ cup shredded unsweetened coconut, toasted

In a saucepan, combine the chile half, water, sugar, ginger, vanilla, lime zest, orange zest, and spearmint. Over low heat, simmer for 5 minutes. Turn off the heat and allow the mixture to steep for 30 minutes. Strain the mixture through a sieve and chill the liquid in the refrigerator for at least an hour.

Combine all the fruit in a bowl and mix well. To serve, spoon the fruit into 4 chilled soup bowls. Add the chilled liquid over the fruits and garnish with the coconut.

PINEAPPLE AND PEAR SALAD WITH SPICED HONEY-LEMON DRESSING

Yield: 8 servings

Heat Scale: Medium

As with any fruit salad, substitutions are easy to make, and the dressing will spice up just about any combination imaginable. Serve this salad over fresh mixed greens.

1 ripe pineapple, peeled, cored, and chopped

2 large ripe pears, peeled, cored, and chopped

2 oranges, peeled, seeded, and chopped

$^{1}/_{4}$ cup pineapple juice

2 tablespoons honey

2 tablespoons lemon juice

$^{1}/_{4}$ cup vegetable oil

$^{1}/_{2}$ teaspoon poppy seeds

1 red jalapeño chile, stemmed, seeded, and minced

Combine the pineapple, pears, and oranges in a bowl, toss gently, and set aside. In a jar, combine the pineapple juice, honey, lemon juice, vegetable oil, poppy seeds, and chile. Cover tightly and shake vigorously. Pour the dressing over the fruit mixture and toss gently. Cover and chill for 1 to 24 hours.

RUJAK (SPICY INDONESIAN FRUIT SALAD)

Yield: 8 servings

Heat Scale: Mild

Jeff Corydon collected this recipe for us in Padang, and it was first published in Chile Pepper *magazine. He noted, "The secret of this spicy salad is in the sauce, and almost any firm fleshy fruit will do. Others that could be used include underripe bananas, carambolas (star fruit), Asian pears, and some vegetables such as jicama or even cucumbers. Rujak of various sorts is eaten all over Indonesia, but Padang's recipe honors local taste by including crushed peanuts and additional chiles in the sauce." Trassi (shrimp paste) is available in Asian markets. If you can't find it, substitute anchovy paste. Note: This recipe requires advance preparation.*

5 cups water

1 teaspoon salt

1 pomelo or tart pink grapefruit, peeled and sectioned

2 slightly underripe mangoes, peeled and cut in
   bite-sized pieces

2 tart apples, peeled and cut in bite-sized pieces

1 small pineapple, peeled and cut in bite-sized pieces

4 red serrano chiles or jalapeños, seeds and
   stems removed, chopped

$^1/_4$ teaspoon trassi

$^1/_2$ teaspoon salt

2 tablespoons dried tamarind pulp

$^1/_4$ cup palm sugar (gula jawa) or dark brown sugar

$^1/_2$ cup unsalted roasted peanuts, crushed, or
   $^1/_4$ cup crunchy peanut butter

Mix 4 cups of the water with 1 teaspoon of salt and soak the pomelo, mangoes, apples, and pineapple overnight in the refrigerator.

Place the chiles, trassi, and $^1/_2$ teaspoon of salt in a blender or food processor and blend until smooth.

Make "tamarind water" by mashing the dried tamarind in 2 tablespoons of hot water until it softens and dissolves. Strain the mixture to remove any seeds or clots.

Melt the gula jawa in a pan with the remaining 1 cup water over low heat until the sugar dissolves, about 5 to 10 minutes. Add the crushed peanuts, chile pepper mixture, and tamarind water, and simmer for 5 minutes more, stirring often, until a fairly thick, sticky syrup forms. Chill the syrup.

To serve, drain the water from the fruits. Pour the syrup over them and toss with a spoon to coat evenly. Serve at once.

BUTTERSCORCH LEMON SAUCE

Yield: About $1^1/_2$ cups
Heat Scale: Medium

This sauce is wonderful when served over poached pears, apple slices, fresh strawberries, raspberries, or even vanilla ice cream.

5 tablespoons butter
1 cup firmly packed brown sugar
$^1/_3$ cup heavy cream
$^1/_2$ teaspoon habanero chile powder
1 tablespoon plus 1 teaspoon lemon juice

Melt the butter in a saucepan and add the sugar. Stir until sugar dissolves and add the cream and chile powder. Continue cooking over medium heat, stirring occasionally, until the mixture comes to a boil and is thick. Stir in lemon juice and remove from heat. Allow to cool slightly before serving.

CAYENNE-CURRIED APPLES

Yield: 6 servings

Heat Scale: Medium

So call it a firm chutney, but this side dish is more than a relish when the apples retain their shape and texture. Spiced up with curry powder and chile powder, these apples make a daring and delightful accompaniment to roasted or grilled meats.

2 tablespoons butter

$1^{1}/_{2}$ teaspoons imported Indian curry powder

$^{1}/_{8}$ teaspoon ground cinnamon

$^{1}/_{2}$ teaspoon cayenne powder

$^{1}/_{8}$ teaspoon ground ginger

$^{1}/_{4}$ teaspoon salt

2 tablespoons diced onion

$^{1}/_{4}$ cup diced celery

1 tablespoon flour

$^{1}/_{2}$ cup chicken stock

3 unpeeled Granny Smith apples,
  quartered and cored

$^{1}/_{2}$ teaspoon granulated sugar or to taste

Preheat the oven to 375°.

Melt the butter in a small saucepan. Stir in the curry powder, cinnamon, cayenne, ginger, salt, onion, and celery. Cook until vegetables are tender, about 5 minutes. Blend in the flour, stirring well. Add the chicken stock and cook until slightly thickened.

Place the apples in a 1-quart casserole. Sprinkle with sugar. Pour the curry sauce over apples and bake, covered, for 45 minutes or until tender when pierced with a fork. Uncover 5 minutes before the cooking time is up. Allow to cool slightly before serving.

WATERMELON-CHILE SALSA

Yield: 6 cups

Heat Scale: Mild

Peter Zimmer served this to us when he was chef at the Inn of the Anasazi in Santa Fe. It can be served over greens or as an accompaniment to grilled poultry and fish. To rehydrate the pasillas, soak them in hot water for at least 1 hour.

8 pasilla chiles, stemmed, seeded, rehydrated, and julienned

4 cups very ripe watermelon, seeded and diced

1 red onion, sliced

2 tablespoons minced fresh cilantro

$^1/_4$ cup champagne vinegar

$^1/_4$ cup extra virgin olive oil

3 plum tomatoes, quartered

Salt and pepper to taste

Combine all the ingredients in a bowl and toss well. Season to taste and chill well (at least 1 hour in the refrigerator), covered, before serving.

THE PERFECT FRUIT?

"No fruit is more to our English taste than the Apple. Let the Frenchman have his Pear, the Italian his Fig, the Jamaican may retain his farinaceous Banana, the Malay his Durian, but for us the Apple. What fruit can compare with the Apple for its extended season, lasting from August to June, keeping alive for us in winter, in its sustained flush and rustic russet, the memory of golden autumnal days? Through all the seven ages of man it finds a welcome, and we now lean that not only does it keep the doctor from our doors, but ourselves from the dentist. Is there another edible which at once is an insurance, a pleasure, and an economy?"

—Edward Bunyard

FRESH FRUIT-HABANERO TOPPING

Yield: 5 cups

Heat Scale: Medium

This topping can also be used over pancakes, waffles, or French toast for an exciting breakfast feast. Feel free to go all out and top the salsa with whipped cream.

2 cups granulated sugar

1 cup water

$^1/_2$ habanero chile

1 cup each diced fresh kiwifruit, peaches, strawberries, and mangoes or other fruit in season

Ice cream of choice or a daring selection from Chapter 10

Combine the sugar and water in a saucepan and bring to a boil. Add the chile half and boil until syrupy, about 10 minutes. Remove the habanero. If you want the syrup hotter, add a little more chile and let sit a few hours before using. Add the diced fruit to the syrup, mix well, and serve over ice cream.

HABANERO-INFUSED
TROPICAL FRUITS WITH RUM

Yield: 6 servings

Heat Scale: Medium

This is our favorite combination of tropical fruits, but considering all the options, cooks should feel free to make substitutions based on seasonal availability. Guavas and exotic citrus fruits such as Jamaican ortaniques are candidates for this salad.

1 habanero chile, seeds and stem removed, minced

1 ripe mango, peeled and diced

2 ripe bananas, peeled and diced

1 ripe papaya, peeled and diced

$^{1}/_{2}$ pineapple, peeled, cored, and diced

Juice of 3 limes

$^{1}/_{4}$ cup dark rum

Combine the chile, mango, banana, papaya, and pineapple with the lime juice and rum in a large bowl and mix well. Chill and allow to marinate for at least 30 minutes.

FRUIT KEBABS WITH PEPPER JELLY YOGURT SAUCE

Yield: 24

🔥 🔥

Heat Scale: Medium

The cooling yogurt and the hot pepper jelly battle it out in the sauce that tops these fruit kebabs. Feel free to add mangoes, papayas, and bananas to the skewers. The sauce and the fruit kebabs may be made 1 day in advance and kept covered and chilled.

1 cup plain yogurt

2 teaspoons granulated sugar

$^1/_8$ teaspoon vanilla extract

1 teaspoon Scotch Bonnet Pepper Jelly (page 85)

1 pineapple, peeled, cored, and cubed

3 kiwifruits, peeled and sliced

2 pints strawberries, hulled

1 honeydew melon, cleaned and cubed

24 (6-inch) wooden skewers

In a bowl, whisk together the yogurt, sugar, vanilla, and pepper jelly. Allow to chill in the refrigerator for at least 1 hour.

Thread the fruits on the skewers, alternating the pineapple, kiwifruits, strawberries, and the honeydew. Serve the fruit kebabs with the sauce ladled over them.

THE WONDERS OF PINEAPPLES

• *A pineapple was grown indoors in 1642 in the Duchess of Cleveland's greenhouse and was presented to King Charles II.*

• *The pineapple is not really a fruit but is a collection of berries.*

• *Farmers in Benin, Africa, developed a variety of pineapple that was too large to market.*

• *Some diet specialists suggest that the chemical bromelin in pineapples, when the fruit is eaten on an empty stomach, will consume fat. Trouble is, dieters were expected to consume 4 pounds of pineapples in 2 days.*

BALSAMIC STRAWBANEROS
WITH MINTED CREAM

Yield: 4 servings

Heat Scale: Medium

Forget peaches and cream! Here's a summer dessert selection you'll want to serve over and over again. The tartness of the strawberries works well with the sweet cream and habanero heat.

1 pint sweet strawberries, washed and quartered

$^1/_2$ cup balsamic vinegar

$^1/_2$ cup loosely packed brown sugar

2 tablespoons freshly chopped mint leaves

$^1/_4$ fresh habanero chile, stemmed, seeded, and minced

MINTED CREAM

$^1/_2$ cup heavy whipping cream

2 tablespoons granulated sugar

1 tablespoon freshly chopped mint leaves

Set aside the strawberries in a bowl the refrigerator.

In a medium mixing bowl, combine the balsamic vinegar with the brown sugar and keep tasting until you achieve a sweet-and-sour taste to your liking. Add 2 tablespoons of the mint and the habanero, stir, and pour the mixture over the strawberries. Allow strawberries to marinate for at least 30 minutes.

Whip the heavy cream with a wire whisk in a medium bowl. As the cream starts to form peaks, add the granulated sugar, then the remaining tablespoon of mint. To serve, spoon the strawberries into a bowl with a little of the marinade, and top with a dollop of the Minted Cream.

STRAWBERRIES WITH TEX-MEX TEQUILA AND BLACK PEPPER

Yield: 6 servings

Heat Scale: Mild

This is a shocking dessert if there ever was one, with the sharp flavors of the pepper tequila and black pepper strangely complementing the sweetness of the strawberries. Only a truly daring chilehead would serve this over one of our chile ice creams in Chapter 10.

6 cups halved strawberries

$^1/_2$ cup orange juice

$^1/_4$ cup Tex-Mex Tequila (page 156)

2 teaspoons freshly ground black pepper

2 teaspoons balsamic vinegar

Mint sprigs for garnish

Combine the strawberries, orange juice, tequila, black pepper, and balsamic vinegar in a bowl and toss well. Cover and chill for 3 hours, stirring occasionally. Spoon the mixture into 6 small glass bowls and garnish with the mint sprigs.

PEAR COMPOTE IN A
CRANBERRY-HABANERO NECTAR

Yield: 8 servings
Heat Scale: Medium

A compote is a fruit that is slowly cooked in a sugar syrup so as to retain its shape. (However, we can't promise you'll retain your shape after consuming these pears.) Serve the pears warm or cold as an accompaniment for poultry or as a dessert.

2 cups fresh cranberries

1 teaspoon stemmed, seeded, and minced
   fresh habanero chile

1 cup fresh orange juice

1 cup granulated sugar

4 large fresh pears, peeled, cored, and halved

Preheat the oven to 350°.

Combine the cranberries, habanero, orange juice, and sugar in a saucepan and stir well. Cook over medium heat, stirring constantly, until the berries start to pop. Simmer for 3 minutes. Remove from the heat and pour into a shallow baking pan.

Place the pear halves in the cranberry mixture. Cover and bake for about 30 minutes or until pears are just tender, turning once. Serve the pears with the cranberry-habanero mixture spooned over them.

ORANGES IN FIERY SYRUP
WITH TOASTED COCONUT

Yield: 4 to 6 servings
Heat Scale: Medium

Remember to remove the habanero. (Habaneros are often orange colored, and mistaking one for a piece of an orange could have serious consequences.) Toasting the coconut is optional, but it gives an added, nutty flavor. Serve this dessert with snifters of cognac.

1 cup freshly squeezed orange juice

$^1/_4$ cup freshly squeezed lemon juice

$^1/_2$ cup granulated sugar

$^1/_{16}$ teaspoon salt

$^1/_2$ fresh habanero chile, stemmed and seeded

2 cups fresh orange sections, well cleaned

$^1/_2$ cup grated fresh coconut

Combine the orange juice, lemon juice, sugar, salt, and chile half in a saucepan, stir well, and bring to a boil. Boil for 5 minutes. Add the orange sections and boil for 1 minute longer. Remove from heat and place saucepan in a cold water bath to chill the mixture. Remove the habanero. Transfer the oranges and syrup to a serving bowl, cover, and chill in the refrigerator for at least 1 hour.

Toast the coconut in a dry skillet, stirring with a wooden spoon, until the coconut is lightly browned. Serve the orange sections in glass bowls with the toasted coconut sprinkled on top.

ORANGES AND PINEAPPLE
IN LEMON-SERRANO SYRUP

Yield: 6 servings

Heat Scale: Medium

When stored in an antique jar, this dessert makes a very attractive presentation at the table. For even more color, don't strain the red chile from the syrup.

6 small navel or Valencia oranges

1 large, ripe pineapple

2 cups granulated sugar

$^{1}/_{2}$ cup lemon juice

3 cups water

2 red serrano or jalapeño chiles, stemmed, seeded, and minced

$^{1}/_{4}$ cup apple brandy

Spearmint sprigs for garnish

Peel the oranges and remove all the white pith, but leave them whole. Cut off the top of the pineapple, cut it lengthwise into halves and then in quarters. Use a sharp knife inserted between the flesh and the skin to pare the pineapple quarters, cutting away the "eyes." Slice each pineapple quarter in half.

Bring the sugar, lemon juice, and water to a boil in a saucepan. Lower the heat and simmer the syrup for 15 minutes. Add the oranges, pineapple segments, and serrano chiles and simmer for 10 more minutes, turning the fruits once or twice so that they poach evenly. Remove the fruits and place them in a glass jar with a lid.

Continue to cook the syrup over brisk heat another 10 to 15 minutes, until it becomes slightly syrupy. Remove from heat and cool. Strain through a fine sieve into the jar with the fruits; add the brandy and mix gently.

To serve, spoon 1 whole orange and a segment of pineapple into individual dishes and add a little of the syrup. Garnish with the spearmint sprigs. Leftover fruit should be stored in the jar in the refrigerator.

PEARS QUEMADO

Yield: 6 servings

Heat Scale: Medium

This recipe is from the legendary John Philips Cranwell, hilarious author of the first collection of hot and spicy recipes, The Hellfire Cookbook. *Alas, it is long out of print, but we can still enjoy John's dessert. He wrote of this dish, "Quemado, which means a kind of burned drink, is literally fiery in every sense of the word. I suggest you serve it before or with the coffee. According to a legend, quemado is a lovers' potion. The fire in and on it reflects the fire in their eyes, souls, and bodies. Mayhap 'tis true. Mayhap if after two bowls each they are not stone cold drunk on the floor, they pass the remainder of the night in an ethereal, if fuzzy, lovers' paradise. I can't vouch for the legend, but this is a most unusual dish both in appearance and taste."*

While pears are wonderful in this dessert, you might also try this recipe with other fruits, such as Asian apples, which are available year-round.

2 lemons

1 fresh habanero chile, stemmed, seeded, and cut in half

2 teaspoons granulated sugar

4 whole cloves

1 (4-inch) cinnamon stick

$^2/_3$ cup light Barbados rum

$^2/_3$ cup cognac

6 tablespoons 151-proof Jamaican rum

9 ripe but firm pears

$^1/_2$ cup blanched slivered almonds

Remove the zest from both lemons and place it in a large bowl. Add the chile halves and the juice of the lemons. Add the sugar, cloves, and cinnamon, and stir. Pour in the Barbados rum, the cognac, and the Jamaican rum. Allow this mixture to steep for 20 minutes at room temperature, gently stirring on occasion.

Meanwhile, peel and core 3 of the pears, cut them into 1-inch sections, and set aside. If you are not preparing this dessert right before you serve it, you may want to sprinkle a little bit of lemon juice on the pears to keep them from turning brown. Place the other 6 pears in a large pot filled with boiling water and blanche them for about 15 minutes, or until they appear translucent. When the pears are blanched, carefully remove their skins and place 1 pear on each of the serving plates.

About 15 minutes before you are ready to serve, remove the habanero halves and transfer the liquid mixture to a saucepan. Cover and bring the mixture to a simmer. Divide the sectioned pears among the 6 very warm saucers and sprinkle the blanched almonds over them.

After the contents of the saucepan have simmered about 1 minute, remove the cover, light a match and toss it into the saucepan to ignite the mixture. Let the flames die down a little and ladle the blazing mixture over the pears and almonds. Serve while flames still rise from each dish.

PEARS, PEARS, AND MORE PEARS

"In historic times, one of the most astonishing phenomena we note about the pear is the speed with which it develops new varieties. It enters with remarkable versatility into new combinations and metamorphoses and throws off mutants as a burning brand throws off sparks. Theophrastus mentioned three kinds of pears; Cato recorded five, or possibly six; Pliny, depending on how you translate him, thirty-eight to forty-one; Palladius fifty-six; and Columella said pears were too numerous to list. In seventeenth-century Italy, one catalog named 209 varieties, another gave 232. The British must have been slow in taking up the pear, for they were only cultivating 64 kinds in 1640; but in 1842 there were more than 700, and a catalog of 1868 listed 850."

—Waverly Root

BERRIES AND APRICOTS WITH CHOCOLATE AND CAYENNE CREAM

Yield: 4 servings
Heat Scale: Medium

🔥 🔥

The presentation of this dessert in parfait glasses is quite striking, but be sure to warn guests that the innocent-looking treat is fired-up with cayenne.

CAYENNE CREAM

3 egg yolks

3 tablespoons granulated sugar

$1^1/_2$ cups heavy cream

$^1/_2$ teaspoon cayenne powder

1 teaspoon vanilla extract

---

1 pint raspberries, blackberries, or strawberries

$^1/_3$ pound dried apricots, chopped

2 ounces semisweet chocolate, finely chopped

$^1/_2$ cup chopped pistachios

Whisk the egg yolks and sugar in a large bowl until pale yellow. Heat the cream in a saucepan until it just comes to a simmer. Gradually whisk the hot cream and cayenne into the egg yolk mixture. Return mixture to saucepan and cook over low heat, stirring constantly with a wooden spoon, until the mixture is slightly thickened and lightly coats the back of a spoon, about 8 minutes. (Do not to boil the mixture.) Add the vanilla, pour into a bowl, and chill.

Layer the fruits and chocolate into 4 parfait glasses: first the berries, then the apricots, and then the chocolate. If not serving immediately, refrigerate at this point.

To serve, pour the cream mixture over the fruits and top with the pistachios.

BANANAS IN RUM FLAMBÉ

Yield: 8 to 10 servings
Heat Scale: Mild

The very recipe title of this banana dessert conjures up memories for Dave. His parents, Dick and Barbara, regularly prepared it—without the chile—in the late 1950s. As kids, Dave and his brother Rick were entranced with the idea of setting food on fire. Sometimes if they were out of rum, Dick would substitute brandy or even blended whiskey. The bananas were always served with vanilla ice cream. Variation: Sprinkle the bananas with toasted coconut.

$^1/_4$ cup butter, melted
$^3/_4$ cup loosely packed brown sugar
1 teaspoon finely ground New Mexican red chile,
  such as Chimayó
5 firm bananas, peeled and sliced lengthwise
$^3/_4$ cup dark rum
Ground allspice

Combine the butter, sugar, and chile in a large skillet and stir over low heat. Add the bananas and cook gently until they are just soft, turning once. Add the dark rum and allow it to heat for 1 to 2 minutes. Throw a lighted match into the skillet and set the bananas aflame. When the flame dies out, transfer the bananas to serving plates, spoon some of the sauce over them, and sprinkle with the allspice.

FIG BANANAS BAKED IN A
CITRUS-CHILE MARMALADE GLAZE

Yield: 5 servings

Heat Scale: Medium

Fig bananas are the small bananas also known as frog bananas in parts of the Caribbean. They can be found in Latin or Asian markets in North America. Serve this dessert with the finest sipping rum or mescal.

10 fig bananas, peeled

$^{1}/_{4}$ cup Five-Citrus, Two-Chile Marmalade (page 83)

2 tablespoons honey

1 tablespoon melted butter

Freshly ground allspice or nutmeg

Preheat the oven to 450°.

Place the bananas in a lightly buttered 8 by 8-inch baking dish. In a small saucepan, combine the marmalade, honey, and butter and stir over low heat until well mixed. Pour this over the bananas, coating well. Bake for 10 to 12 minutes.

Arrange the bananas on dessert plates and spoon the marmalade syrup in the pan over each. Sprinkle with allspice and serve.

TANGERINES WITH CINNAMON, CAYENNE, AND CHOCOLATE

Yield: 5 servings

Heat Scale: Medium

This simple dessert can be made in a matter of minutes, but takes a little while to chill and for the flavors to combine. Small oranges or even grapefruits may substituted.

6 tangerines, separated into segments

$^1/_4$ cup tangerine or orange juice

$1^1/_2$ teaspoons granulated sugar

$^1/_4$ teaspoon ground cinnamon

$^1/_2$ teaspoon cayenne powder

$^1/_2$ ounce Mexican chocolate (such as Ibarra) or semisweet chocolate, finely shaved

In a bowl, combine the tangerines, juice, sugar, cinnamon, and cayenne and mix well. Cover and refrigerate until chilled, about 1 hour. Spoon the tangerines and liquid into individual bowls, sprinkle with the shaved chocolate, and serve.

SPICED APPLE AND
ORANGE SAUCE

Yield: About 2 cups

Heat Scale: Medium

This sauce, served over breakfast breads, rolls, or scones, will get any-one's attention. It also makes a great topping for ice cream.

4 large tart cooking apples, peeled, cored, and chopped

2 large oranges, peeled and chopped

$^1/_2$ cup water

$^1/_2$ cup granulated sugar

$^1/_8$ teaspoon salt

$^1/_8$ teaspoon ground cloves

$^1/_2$ teaspoon stemmed, seeded, and minced
fresh habanero chile

Combine the apples, oranges, and water in a saucepan. Cover and cook over medium heat until tender, about 10 minutes. Remove from the heat and stir in remaining ingredients. Mash with a fork and stir well to make a sauce, adding a little water if needed. Return to the heat and cook, uncovered, for 2 minutes.

SWEET AND HOT STRAWBERRY
BARBECUE SAUCE

Yield: 2 cups
Heat Scale: Mild

From the California Strawberry Festival, held in Oxnard, comes this winning recipe from Roxanne E. Chan of Albany, California. First published in Chile Pepper *magazine, it can be used right from the blender to marinate meat, fish, or mushrooms before grilling. Or, you can also simmer the sauce in an uncovered saucepan until thickened before basting ribs, chicken, or steaks.*

2 cups fresh strawberries, hulled and sliced

$^1/_3$ cup strawberry preserves

$^1/_3$ cup ketchup

2 tablespoons soy sauce

2 tablespoons lemon juice

1 large garlic clove, minced

1 teaspoon chopped fresh ginger

$^1/_2$ teaspoon cayenne powder

$^1/_2$ teaspoon grated lemon zest

1 green onion, minced

2 tablespoons chopped fresh cilantro

Place all ingredients in a food processor or blender and purée until smooth.

9

▲▲

DANGEROUS DRINKS

We call these drinks dangerous because many of them contain both chile and alcohol. However, in some cases the alcohol can simply be omitted—but that also means that flaming drinks won't ignite!

The combination of alcohol and spicy flavors is not new. Interestingly, chile pepper-flavored liquors originated in a country virtually devoid of fiery foods: Russia. The word vodka is the Russian diminutive for "water," which gives a fairly good indication of just how basic and important this liquor is in the former Soviet Union. In fact, the people there love it so much they cannot leave it alone. They blend about forty different flavors of various herbs and spices with their vodkas, including combinations of heather, mint, nutmeg, cloves, cinnamon—and, of course, cayenne.

A favorite brand of Russian chile pepper vodka is Stolichnaya Pertsovka, the famous "Stoly," which has been infused with white and black pepper combined with cayenne powder and then filtered to remove all solids. Unfortunately, the reddish tint of the vodka is the result of added caramel coloring rather than the chiles, but it still tastes great and has a nice bite. Other popular brands of hot vodkas are Absolut Peppar from Sweden and America's own Gordon's Pepper Flavored Vodka.

The success of the flavored vodkas has led liquor distillers to experiment with other combinations of alcohol and chile peppers. A few years ago, Brittany Importers in Miami introduced Fire God, nicknamed the "Tequilapeño" because it is a combination of tequila and jalapeños. Another such product is New Mexico Green Chile Wine, produced by Sandia Shadows Vineyard and Winery in Albuquerque. The wine has the flavor of the green chile but only slight heat. In our area, both Fire God and New Mexico Green Chile Wine are used to create spicy variations on margaritas and other fruit-juiced cocktails.

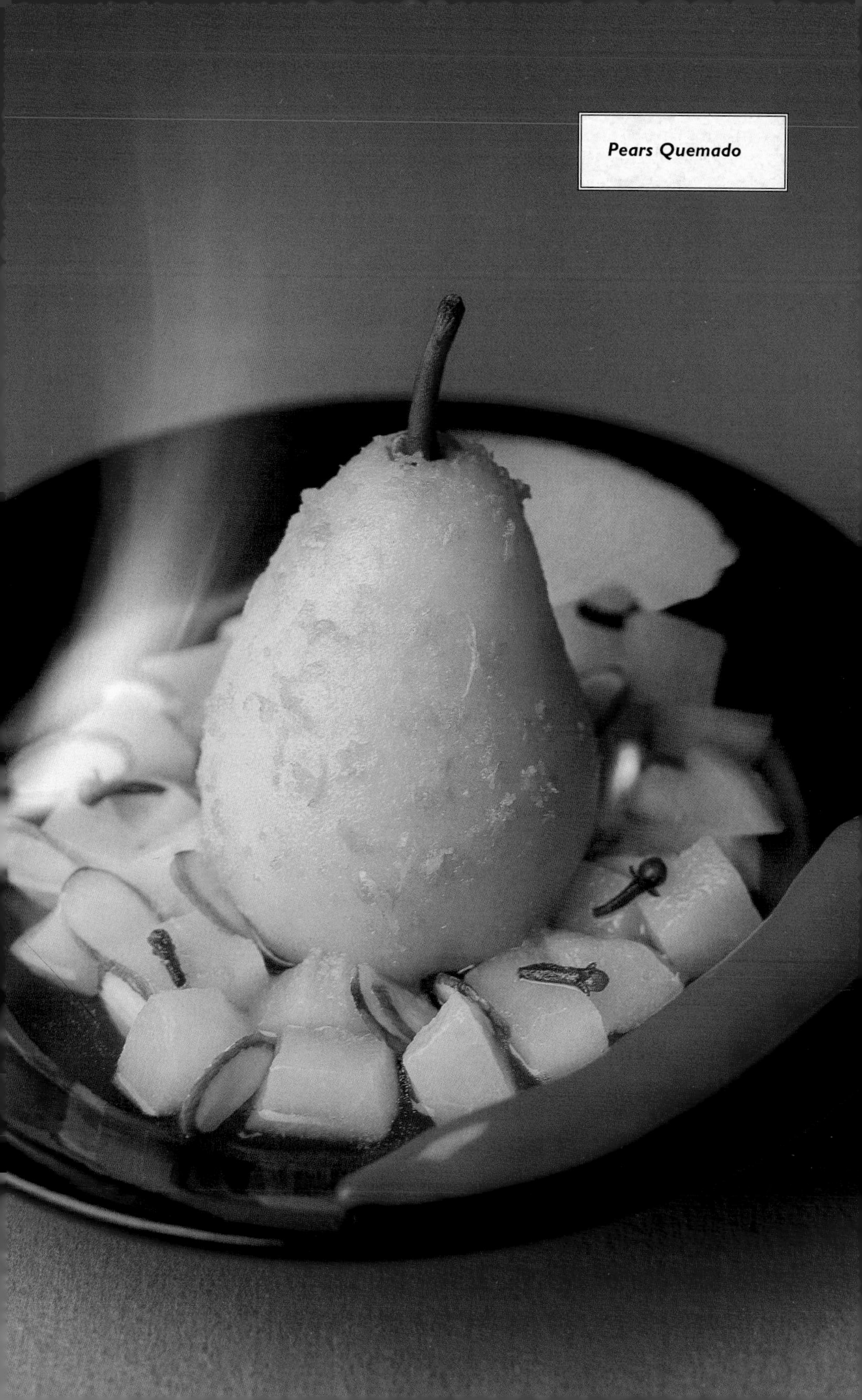

Pears Quemado

New Mexican Hot Chocolate (left)
and Fiery Frozen Margarita with
Red Chile Salt (right)

We have provided two recipes for chile liquors for people who like to create their own. Tex-Mex Tequila (page 156) and Jalapeño Vodka (page 159) can be served chilled or used in cocktails and other recipes in this book. The ideal way to introduce guests to these spicy liquors is to place the bottle in the freezer for a few hours. The liquor becomes thick but does not freeze, and should be served straight-up. (Remember to warn your guests that these cocktails are fiery as well as frosty.) For added fun, present the tequila or vodka with the bottle frozen in a solid block of ice.

The pungent principle at work in the near-frozen pepper vodkas is the reverse of cooked foods. Warming increases the intensity of the aromas of foods, while cooling reduces them. The opposite occurs with the chile pepper vodkas; when the temperature of vodka rises above freezing, the aroma and flavor dissipate—the same is true of ice creams and sorbets. We often think of frozen or thick fruit drinks as cool-downs, but the intriguing chile heat of our blistering beverages rates them as "cool-ups." And, of course, we've included a couple of "hot and healthy" drinks.

A BEVERAGE FIT FOR AN AZTEC EMPEROR

"The emperor [Moctezuma] took no other beverage than the chocolatl, a potation of chocolate, flavoured with vanilla and other spices, and so prepared as to be reduced to a froth of the consistency of honey, which gradually dissolved in the mouth. This beverage, if so it could be called, was served in golden goblets, with spoons of the same metal or of tortoise shell finely wrought. The emperor was exceedingly fond of it, to judge from the quantity—no less than fifty jars or pitchers—prepared for his own daily consumption. Two thousand more were allowed for that of his household."

—William Prescott, History Of The Conquest Of Mexico

TEX-MEX TEQUILA

Yield: 1 liter

Heat Scale: Varies, but usually hot

Nearly any small, red chile pepper can be used in this recipe, but the chiltepins (called "chilipiquins" in Texas) work particularly well because they are small enough that the whole pod can fit through the neck of the bottle. Flavored liquors are often prepared in the Southwest with sliced jalapeños, too. Obviously, the longer the chiles are left in, the hotter the tequila will be! Serve extremely cold in shot glasses, over ice, or in tomato juice for an "instant" Bloody Maria. Tex-Mex Tequila will keep indefinitely in a cool, dark place. Note: This recipe requires advance preparation.

6 dried whole chiltepin chiles or any small, hot
   dried chiles, stemmed

1 liter white tequila (Herradura preferred)

Place the chiltepins in the tequila, seal the bottle, and let them steep for a week or more. Periodically taste the liquor and remove the chiles when the desired heat has been obtained.

CAFE DIABLE

Yield: Four 12-ounce servings
Heat Scale: Mild

At last, what to do with that chafing dish you couldn't give away at your last yard sale. Use it to make this flaming coffee that is also known as café brûlée. However, it is doubtful that the French would spice it up quite as much as we do. This recipe is adapted from one by John Philips Cranwell.

1 large wide piece lemon zest
1 large wide piece orange zest
5 small (granulated) sugar cubes
$^1/_4$ teaspoon ground cloves
$^1/_4$ teaspoon ground cinnamon
1 teaspoon finely ground ancho or pasilla chile
$^1/_4$ teaspoon vanilla extract
$1^1/_2$ cups cognac
3 cups strong hot coffee
4 small twists lemon zest

Combine the wide pieces of lemon and orange zest, the 4 sugar cubes, cloves, cinnamon, ground chile, vanilla, and cognac in the bottom pan of chafing dish and bring to a simmer over low heat. Put a large ladle into the mixture until the ladle is hot, a matter of a few seconds. Fill the ladle almost full with the mixture and add reserved sugar cube. Ignite the mixture in the ladle. When it is burning well, return contents of the ladle to the chafing dish. This will set the mixture afire. Add the hot coffee to the chafing dish and mix well. When the flame has subsided, pour the coffee into the small cups in which you've placed the twists of lemon zest.

NEW MEXICAN
HOT CHOCOLATE

Yield: Six 4-ounce servings
Heat Scale: Medium

As this drink moved up from Mexico to New Mexico, it gained considerable heat with the addition of New Mexican red chile. Traditionally the hot chocolate is beaten at the table with a molinillo, a carved wooden stirrer that is rubbed between the palms, made specifically for preparing hot chocolate. Molinillos are available in Mexican specialty shops. Serve this in heavy earthenware mugs—preferably emblazoned with chile peppers.

- $1/3$ cup unsweetened cocoa
- 1 tablespoon flour
- $1/3$ cup granulated sugar
- $3/4$ teaspoon ground cinnamon
- $1/4$ teaspoon ground cloves
- 1 teaspoon finely ground New Mexican red chile
- 1 cup water
- 2 cups half-and-half
- 1 cup milk
- $1^1/2$ teaspoons vanilla
- 1 cup whipping cream
- Freshly grated nutmeg
- 6 whole cinnamon sticks

Combine the cocoa, flour, sugar, cinnamon, cloves, and red chile with the water in a large saucepan. Stir or whisk until very blended. Heat until bubbling and just barely beginning to simmer. Gradually add the half-and-half, then the milk in a very fine stream, stirring constantly. Beat with your molinillo or a whisk. Heat until hot, but do not boil, and keep warm for at least 5 minutes.

Whip the cream with the vanilla. Whip the chocolate again just before serving with the molinillo until it is frothy. Top with a dollop of whipped cream and a pinch of nutmeg. Insert a cinnamon stick into the cream and serve.

HOT CHOCOLATE AGASAJO-STYLE

"Food historian Maricel Presilla has re-created a drink served at the lavish receptions called agasajos in 17th-century Spain. Combine $^1/_2$ gallon milk; $^1/_4$ oz. dried rosebuds or 2 tsp. rosewater; 1 tsp. saffron threads, lightly crushed; 3 sticks cinnamon; 2 whole dried árbol or pequín chiles; 1 vanilla bean, split lengthwise; and $^1/_2$ cup sugar in a large, heavy saucepan over medium heat. Scald milk, stirring to dissolve sugar; then lower heat and cook 10 minutes. Remove from heat; steep 10 minutes. Strain into a large pot. Heat gently, then add $^1/_2$ lb. of bittersweet chocolate, coarsely chopped. Whisk briskly for 5 minutes to dissolve chocolate and make a frothy head. Serves 8."

—*Elizabeth Schneider*

JALAPEÑO VODKA

Yield: 1 liter
Heat Scale: Varies, but usually hot

Pepper vodkas are very popular in Russia and Eastern Europe, and also among vodka-loving chileheads. As with the Tex-Mex Vodka in this chapter, the longer the jalapeños steep, the hotter the vodka will be. It's advisable to taste the vodka every day or so to adjust the heat to individual tastes. Jalapeño Vodka will keep indefinitely in a cool, dark place. Note: This recipe requires advance preparation.

4 jalapeño chiles, stemmed, seeded, and quartered
1 liter vodka (Stolichnaya preferred)

Place the jalapeños in the vodka and let sit for a week or more. When the heat level is to your taste, remove the jalapeños and serve in your favorite cocktails.

ANCHO CHILE AND RUM
MULLED CITRUS CIDER

Yield: Ten 8-ounce servings
Heat Scale: Mild

To "mull" a beverage is to heat it with other ingredients to impart a flavor.

8 cups apple cider

1 tablespoon finely ground ancho or pasilla chile

1 lemon, sliced very thin

$^1/_2$ orange, sliced very thin

2 teaspoons lemon juice

4 (3-inch) cinnamon sticks

2 tablespoons whole cloves

2 cups dark rum

Combine all ingredients in a large saucepan and heat but do not bring to a boil. Simmer on low heat for 15 minutes. Strain the mixture through a sieve, pour into mugs, and serve warm.

CHILE-INFUSED
CRANBERRY CIDER

Yield: Six 8-ounce servings
Heat Scale: Medium ◊ ◊

Here's another mulled cider that contains two chiles, the mild ancho and the super-hot habanero. The ancho adds the raisiny overtones and the habanero supplies an additional fruity heat. Serve this cider in large mugs around a roaring fire in the winter.

4 cups apple cider
1 ancho chile, stemmed, seeded, and cut into thin strips
2 cups cranberry juice cocktail
1 teaspoon whole cloves
1 (3-inch) cinnamon stick
$^{1}/_{2}$ habanero chile, stemmed and seeded
Ground nutmeg or allspice for garnish

Combine the cider, ancho chile strips, and cranberry juice cocktail in a large bowl and let sit for 30 minutes. Transfer to a large saucepan, add the cloves, cinnamon stick, and chile half and bring to a boil. Reduce the heat and simmer, uncovered, for 10 minutes.

Remove from the heat, strain, and pour into mugs. Sprinkle some nutmeg over each mug.

FRESH PEACH AND CHILE DAIQUIRIS

Yield: Four 8-ounce servings
Heat Scale: Mild

For some reason, habanero chiles work particularly well with fruits. These daiquiris will delight chileheads, who will probably suggest adding more habanero to the blender. For a nonalcoholic version of this drink, substitute pineapple juice for the rum and decrease the sugar to 3 tablespoons.

2 cups fresh peach slices

$^1/_4$ cup freshly squeezed lime juice

$^1/_2$ teaspoon stemmed, seeded, and minced fresh habanero chile

1 cup dark rum

$^1/_3$ cup granulated sugar

1 cup crushed ice

Mint sprigs

In a blender, combine the peaches, lime juice, and chile and purée. Add the rum, sugar, and crushed ice and purée until smooth. Pour into stemmed glasses and garnish with mint sprigs.

FIERY YET FROZEN MARGARITA
WITH RED CHILE SALT

Yield: Four 6-ounce servings
Heat Scale: Medium

Here is a drink with enough basic flavors to please anyone, being sweet, hot, salty, and sour at the same time. Use small spherical key limes, if possible. Variation: For a milder margarita with the flavor of green chile, substitute New Mexico Green Chile Wine for the fiery tequila.

6 to 8 fresh limes, or enough to make $^{1}/_{2}$ cup juice

Salt

$1^{1}/_{2}$ cups Tex-Mex Tequila (see recipe, page 156)

$^{1}/_{3}$ cup Cointreau or Triple Sec

Crushed ice

RED CHILE SALT

2 tablespoons salt

1 teaspoon New Mexican red chile powder

4 lime slices for garnish

Juice the limes, reserve the juice, and save 1 lime section.

Place the lime juice, tequila, and Cointreau or Triple Sec in a blender. Add the crushed ice until the blender is half full and then process. Taste the result and adjust the flavors by adding more Cointreau to make it sweeter, more lime juice to make it more tart, more tequila to increase the heat level, or more ice to decrease the heat level.

Combine the salt and Chile powder on plate. Prepare 4 long-stemmed goblets by rubbing the rims with the remaining lime section. Dip the goblet rims in the salt and then place in the freezer for at least 30 minutes. Pour the margarita mix into the frosted goblets and garnish with a slice of lime.

SANGRITA DE CHAPALA

Yield: About 3 cups
Heat Scale: Medium

This particular version of sangrita, *or "bloody little drink," comes from Chapala, Mexico, where the bartenders have not succumbed to the temptation of adding tomato juice to this concoction, as the gringos do. The bloody color comes from the grenadine, so this is truly a sweet heat drink that is also salty. Some people take a sip of tequila after each swallow of* sangrita, *while others mix 1 part tequila to 4 parts sangrita to make a cocktail. Sangrita de Chapala will keep for 1 week in the refrigerator.*

2 cups orange juice

³/₄ cup grenadine syrup

2 teaspoons Mexican hot sauce or any habanero hot sauce

1 tablespoon salt

Combine all ingredients in a jar, shake well, and chill.

THE ESSENCE OF SANGRITA

"A good sangrita is made from the juice of freshly squeezed tart oranges, sweetened slightly with grenadine (a syrup flavored with pomegranates) and spiced with salsa made from the fiery puya chile. The resulting concoction, with its sweet, sour, and spicy flavors, is a natural compadre for tequila. One Mexican brand of sangrita, called Vuida de Sanchez, is based on the original recipe, purportedly created by Guadelupe Sanchez in the 1930s at Lake Chapala outside of Guadalajara (although many others also boast its invention)."
—Lucinda Hutson

HABANERO-ORANGE WINE

Yield: About 7 cups
Heat Scale: Medium

🔥 🔥

This spiced-up dessert wine is our rather radical variation on a specialty drink from Provence. It can be served ice cold, on the rocks, or mixed with chilled champagne. The wine will keep, chilled, for 6 months. Note: This recipe requires advance preparation.

4 large oranges, washed and each cut into 16 pieces

$^1/_2$ habanero chile, stemmed and seeded

2 (750-ml) bottles dry white wine (Chardonnay preferred)

1 cup granulated sugar

$^1/_4$ cup cognac

2 long strips of orange zest, removed with
    a vegetable peeler

In a large jar, combine the oranges, chile half, and wine. Cover and chill the mixture for 4 or 5 days. Remove oranges and habanero, add the sugar and cognac, and stir mixture until the sugar is dissolved. Strain the mixture through a sieve lined with a double thickness of cheesecloth. Transfer the wine into 2 decorative bottles. Insert a strip of the orange zest into each bottle, cork the bottles, and chill for 2 or 3 days before serving.

CLAUDE BARTHÉ'S
WALNUT WINE

Yield: About 8 cups
Heat Scale: Mild

Another specialty wine from France, adapted from a recipe collected by Robb Walsh that was first published in Chile Pepper *magazine. Robb wrote, "Vin de noix, or walnut wine, is a fortified wine that makes a delightful apéritif with a nutty flavor and sherry-like finish." The ancho chile adds slight heat and a raisiny flavor. The wine will keep for weeks in the refrigerator.* Note: *This recipe requires advance preparation.*

2 (750-ml) bottles red wine

$^1/_2$ (750-ml) bottle Armagnac or brandy

2 cups granulated sugar

12 crushed green walnuts

1 ancho chile, stemmed, seeded, and cut into thin strips

Combine all ingredients in a large jar and mix well. Cover and age the mixture for 1 month. Strain the mixture through a sieve lined with a double thickness of rinsed and squeezed cheesecloth.

BURNING BRANDY ALEXANDER

Yield: Four 6-ounce servings

Heat Scale: Medium 🔥 🔥

A variation on a traditional cocktail, this spicy ice cream delight makes a great dessert drink. For an interesting variation, substitute crème de menthe for the crème de cacao.

$^{1}/_{4}$ cup brandy

$^{1}/_{4}$ cup brown crème de cacao

4 scoops Arizona Chiltepin Ice Cream, slightly softened (page 181)

Ground nutmeg or allspice for garnish

Spearmint leaves for garnish

Place the brandy, crème de cacao, and ice cream in a blender and purée. Serve in dessert glasses and sprinkle with the nutmeg. Garnish each glass with spearmint leaves.

SPICY BOTTLED DRINKS

Successes

- *Cave Creek Chili Beer, with a whole serrano chile in each bottle.*
- *New Mexico Green Chile Wine, which features the state vegetable.*

Failures

- *Cajun Cola, a spicy soft drink from Louisiana flavored with cola, cinnamon, and hot sauce.*
- *Jalapeño Wine, an early attempt by a company called Domingo and the Gringo.*

MANGO LASSI
WITH HABANERO

Serves: Four 12-ounce servings
Heat Scale: Medium

This refreshing drink originated in India, where it is often served for dessert after a meal of fiery hot curries. We have, of course, spiced up a drink originally designed as a cool-down. Fruits such as pineapple, strawberries, peaches, or pineapples may be added to or substituted for the mangoes.

2 cups plain yogurt

2 cups buttermilk (or substitute milk)

Pulp of two ripe mangoes

Juice of one lemon

2 teaspoons granulated sugar

$^1/_4$ fresh habanero or 1 jalapeño chile, stemmed, seeded, and minced

Place all the ingredients in a blender and process until smooth. Serve in dessert glasses over ice, or freeze until slushy and then serve.

SERRANO-PEACH
HONEY SMOOTHIE

Yield: Four 8-ounce servings
Heat Scale: Mild

Here is a thick frozen juice that is very nearly a sorbet. It would be a "cooler" without the serrano chiles, but maybe it's a "heater" with them. Note: *Requires some advance preparation.*

$1^1/_4$ cups plain yogurt

1 pound ripe peaches, peeled, pitted, sliced

2 tablespoons fresh lemon juice

1 teaspoon stemmed, seeded, and minced fresh serrano or jalapeño chiles

$^1/_4$ cup honey

$^1/_4$ teaspoon vanilla extract

Spearmint leaves for garnish

Divide 1 cup of yogurt among 8 sections of an ice cube tray. Freeze until the yogurt cubes are solid, at least 4 hours. (This can be done 1 day ahead and kept frozen.)

In a food processor or blender, combine the peaches, lemon juice, chiles, honey, and vanilla and process until the mixture is well blended. Add the frozen yogurt cubes and process until mixture is smooth and frothy. Pour into chilled tall glasses and serve garnished with the spearmint leaves.

KILL-A-COLD CAYENNE TEA

Yield: Four 8-ounce servings
Heat Scale: Medium

🔥 🔥

Andy Householder, the owner of Hi-Co Western Products, prescribes the following hot tea for a cold that won't go away. Drink as much as you can and repeat until all of the tea—or your cold—is gone.

- 4 cups water
- 1 teaspoon cayenne powder
- 2 regular beef bouillon cubes
- Granulated sugar to taste

In a medium-sized saucepan, heat the water until boiling, then stir in the cayenne and bouillon cubes. Mix until thoroughly dissolved then cool until the broth is not too hot to drink. Add sugar to taste to individual mugs and pour in the tea.

HOT HABANERO TODDY

Yield: 1 cup
Heat Scale: Hot

🔥 🔥 🔥

Here's another spiced-up remedy, however you can omit the bourbon if you are alcohol-sensitive. This drink is usually taken at bedtime and is reputed to be very beneficial for alleviating bronchial and flu symptoms.

- 2 tablespoons bourbon
- 1 tablespoon honey
- 1 tablespoon lemon juice
- $3/_4$ cup very hot water
- $1/_4$ teaspoon habanero powder

Combine all the ingredients in a mug, stir well, and sip the drink slowly while it's hot.

10

SHOCKING SORBETS & ICE CREAMS

Ice cream probably originated in China around 2000 BC. It next appeared in Italy in the seventeenth century, then in the United States in the early eighteenth century. The U.S. ice cream manufacturing industry began in 1851.

In the early days, ice cream was made by placing the ingredients in a metal container that was surrounded by a wooden bucket containing a freezing mixture of ice and coarse salt. The ingredients were frozen and mixed to break up ice crystals until it was smooth.

Then came the days of commercial ice cream production, when people preferred to buy their ice cream from dairies, grocery stores, and trucks that visited neighborhoods. Next came specialty ice cream stores with gourmet flavors. Nowadays, many people have returned to making ice cream and sorbets at home with ice cream makers, which essentially operate the same way as the old hand-crank machines. The newer machines, however, are made from plastic rather than wood—yet they still have an interior metal container.

Of course, our ices, sorbets, and ice creams feature chile peppers, but putting unusual things in ice cream is not new. In *American Gourmet*, Jane and Michael Stern wrote about the ice creams of the 1960s, when some of the flavorings were avocados and angostura bitters.

CANTALOUPE CHILE ICE

Yield: 6 to 8 servings
Heat Scale: Mild

The sweetness of the fresh red chile is an important element in this ice. Substitute other red chiles, such as jalapeños for a hotter dessert. Other melons may also be used. You will need an ice cream maker for this recipe.

 3 small ripe cantaloupes, peeled, seeded, and chopped

 1 fresh red New Mexican chile, stemmed, seeded, and chopped

 $^1/_4$ cup Midori liqueur or melon-flavored liqueur

 6 tablespoons confectioners' sugar

 Juice of 2 lemons or limes

 Pinch of salt

 Mint sprigs for garnish

Combine the cantaloupe and chile in a food processor and purée. Transfer the puree to a bowl and add the remaining ingredients, stirring well. Transfer the mixture to the ice cream maker and process according to the manufacturer's instructions. Serve in chilled bowls garnished with mint sprigs.

PEQUIN-LEMON GRANITA

Yield: 6 servings

Heat Scale: Hot

🔥 🔥 🔥

Scoops of these icy-spicy lemon crystals with the hot red flecks can be served in wine glasses, and slowly savored. The granita (flavored ice) can also be served between courses of an elaborate dinner. Either way, it should be accompanied by a chilled, crisp Riesling.

- 2 cups granulated sugar
- 2 cups water
- 1 cup freshly squeezed lemon juice
- 5 small fresh red pequin or chiltepin chiles or rehydrated dried pequins or Asian chiles, stemmed, seeded, and finely minced or puréed

Combine the sugar and water in a saucepan, bring to a boil, then lower the heat and simmer for 5 to 6 minutes, or until the sugar has melted. Cool to room temperature. Add the lemon juice and chiles and mix until well blended.

Pour the mixture into ice cube trays or a shallow pan, cover with aluminum foil, and place in the freezer. When the mixture starts to freeze at the edges, remove from the freezer and break it up into ice crystals, using a dull knife or a metal spoon. Return to the freezer. Check again in 30 minutes, and when the mixture begins to freeze, repeat the chopping process. Do this at least once more to ensure that the mixture forms into tiny pellets of lemon ice. At serving time you may need to gently chop the mixture once more if the granita is frozen too solid. Spoon the granita into parfait or wine glasses and serve with cookies.

BLOOD ORANGE-YELLOW HOT SORBET

Yield: 6 servings

🔥 🔥   Heat Scale: Medium

Most blood oranges in our market are imported from the Mediterranean, but some varieties with bright red pulp are grown in California. Use fresh yellow hot wax chiles or substitute a combination of one banana chile and one jalapeño chile. You will need an ice cream maker for this recipe.

> Zest of 2 blood oranges
>
> 4 cups blood orange juice (about 12 to 16 oranges)
>
> 2 yellow wax hot chiles, stemmed, seeded, and chopped
>
> 1 cup granulated sugar
>
> $^1/_4$ cup grated coconut, toasted for garnish

Place the zest in a small bowl and set aside.

Strain the orange juice through a sieve into a bowl. Combine 1 cup of the juice and the chiles in a blender and puree. Return the puree to the rest of the juice. Add the sugar and zest and stir until the sugar is entirely dissolved. Chill in the freezer for 30 minutes. Freeze the mixture in an ice cream maker following manufacturer's instructions. Serve the sorbet garnished with the coconut.

THE ETYMOLOGY OF SORBET

"The word sorbet is from Italian sorbetto, itself borrowed from the Turkish chorbêt which is from the Arabic charât, properly speaking, a fruit drink, or sherbet; 'syrup' is derived from the same word."

—Maguelonne Toussaint-Samat

HEAP-OF-HEAT KEY LIME SORBET

Yield: 6 servings

Heat Scale: Medium   ♨ ♨

Key limes are sometimes hard to find, but check your Latin market. You will need an ice cream maker for this recipe, but you can also pour the mixture into a metal cake pan and freeze it until almost solid, about 6 hours. Then purée it in a blender and serve.

$1^1/_4$ cups granulated sugar

$2^1/_2$ cups water

Lime zest for garnish

1 cup freshly squeezed Key lime juice

$^1/_4$ cup freshly squeezed orange juice

$^1/_2$ teaspoon habanero powder

$^1/_2$ teaspoon powdered gelatin

2 tablespoons cold water

Place lime zest in a small bowl and set aside.

In saucepan, combine the sugar and $2^1/_2$ cups water. Bring to a boil and boil for 5 minutes, without stirring. Remove from heat and stir in the lime juice, orange juice, and habanero powder.

In a small saucepan, sprinkle the gelatin over the 2 tablespoons of cold water. Let stand for 1 minute to soften. Heat until the gelatin is dissolved, then stir into the lime juice mixture. Transfer to a bowl and chill in a freezer 30 minutes.

Freeze in an ice cream maker following the manufacturer's instructions. Serve with a sprinkle of lime zest.

GRAPEFRUIT SORBET WITH
MINT AND JALAPEÑO

Yield: 4 servings

Heat Scale: Medium

Use peppermint or spearmint leaves in this herbally spicy dessert, and serve it with champagne. Other citrus fruits, such as pomelos or blood oranges, will also work. Serve this sorbet in small wine glasses. You will need an ice cream maker for this recipe.

$3/_4$ cup granulated sugar

$1/_2$ cup water

1 jalapeño chile, stemmed, seeded, and minced

2 cups freshly squeezed grapefruit juice

Juice of 1 Key lime

1 tablespoon minced mint leaves

1 egg white, lightly beaten

Whole mint leaves for garnish

Combine the sugar and water in a saucepan, bring to a boil and stir until the sugar dissolves. Remove from the heat and cool.

Combine the minced chile with a $1/_4$ cup of the grapefruit juice in a blender and purée. Add this mixture, the remaining grapefruit juice, the lime, minced mint, and egg white to the syrup in a bowl and mix well. Chill in the freezer for 15 minutes.

Place the mixture in an ice cream maker and follow the manufacturer's instructions. Serve garnished with the whole mint leaves.

MANGO-SCOTCH BONNET SORBET

Yield: 6 to 8 servings

Heat Scale: Hot

🔥 🔥 🔥

There's just something about mangoes and Scotch bonnets that fit together. They're usually combined in chutneys and hot sauces, but here they are married in a hot sorbet that is made without an ice cream maker.

2 large mangoes, peeled and chopped

$^1/_3$ cup honey dissolved in $1^1/_2$ cups warm water

1 Scotch bonnet or habanero chile, stemmed, seeded, and minced

2 tablespoons dark rum

$^1/_4$ cup freshly squeezed lemon juice

Thin slices of mango for garnish

In a food processor or blender, purée the mangoes. Add the honey water and blend the mixture until it is smooth. Pour all but $^1/_2$ cup of the mixture into a bowl. Add the Scotch bonnet chile to the reserved mixture, and blend in the blender until puréed fine. Stir the chile mixture into the mango mixture with the rum and the lemon juice and pour the mixture into 2 ice cube trays without dividers or a wide, shallow bowl. Freeze it in the freezer for 1 to 2 hours, or until it is almost firm. Scoop the sorbet into the food processor, purée it, and return it to the trays or bowl. Freeze the sorbet for 2 to 4 hours, or until it is firm but not hard. Scoop it into dessert glasses and garnish with the mango slices.

JALAPEÑO-APRICOT SORBET
WITH PINE NUTS

Yield: 4 servings
Heat Scale: Medium

Ripe red jalapeños have more sugar than the green, immature pods, and blend better with the apricots. If possible, use genuine piñon nuts, which can be purchased from mail-order sources (see page 189), to garnish this sorbet. If you cannot get piñons, substitute the European variety, which are labeled as pignoli.

1 red jalapeño or serrano chile, stemmed, seeded, and chopped

8 ripe apricots, peeled and pitted

1 cup water

$^{1}/_{4}$ cup Muscat or Sauterne wine

$^{1}/_{2}$ cup granulated sugar

$^{1}/_{4}$ cup whole roasted pine nuts

Combine the jalapeño, apricots, water, muscat, and sugar in a blender and purée until the sugar is completely dissolved. Transfer to a bowl and chill in the freezer $^{1}/_{2}$ hour.

Process the mixture in an ice cream maker according to the manufacturer's instructions. Serve with the pine nuts sprinkled on top.

LOWFAT ORANGE-HABANERO
BUTTERMILK ICE

Yield: 4 servings

Heat Scale: Medium

Okay, okay, here's a lowfat dessert that has only one gram of fat in each serving. Any dried fruit can be substituted for the orange peel. You will need an ice cream maker for this recipe.

2 cups buttermilk

$^1/_3$ cup confectioners' sugar

1 tablespoon Triple Sec liqueur

$^1/_4$ cup dried orange peel

$^1/_4$ teaspoon habanero powder

In a bowl, combine the buttermilk and the sugar and beat with an electric mixer until the sugar has dissolved and the mixture is frothy. Beat in the liqueur. Crush the orange peel in a mortar and add it and the habanero powder to the mixture. Beat again. Chill for 1 hour in the freezer.

Process the mixture in an ice cream maker according to manufacturer's instructions.

SNAKEBITE SHERBET

Yield: About 1 gallon

Heat Scale: Hot

*This recipe by Tamlyn Wedlow was a winner at the annual Fire &
Spice Festival held near the hamlet of Inlet in the central Adirondack
Mountains of New York State. Note: This recipe uses an ice cream
maker and requires advance preparation.*

Zest of 3 limes

4 cups water

2 cups granulated sugar

$^1/_2$ cup freshly squeezed lime juice

5 jalapeños, stemmed, seeded, and minced

6 tablespoons tequila

4 egg whites

1 cup heavy cream

In a saucepan, combine the zest of 2 limes with the water and the
sugar. Simmer for 10 minutes, then let the liquid cool to room temperature. Pour the mixture in to a medium mixing bowl, add the remaining
zest, the lime juice, jalapeños, and tequila. Cover and refrigerate for at least
24 hours to let the flavors blend.

The next day, beat the egg whites
in a separate bowl until they are
frothy, but not dry, and combine with
the heavy cream and the refrigerated
mixture. Let sit for 2 hours.

Pour the liquid into the ice cream
maker and follow the manufacturer's
instructions.

**WHY DOES ICE CREAM HAVE
SO MUCH SUGAR?**

*"The coldness of the ice cream numbs our taste
buds, diminishing their sensitivity. In order to
make the ice cream taste sweet, the producer
must use twice as much sugar as it would if
the ice cream were meant to be served at room
temperature. Sugar serves another purpose: It
lowers the freezing point of the ice-cream
mixture and therefore decreases the possibility
that ice crystals will form."*

—Howard Hillman

ARIZONA CHILTEPIN ICE CREAM

Yield: 20 or more servings
Heat Scale: Hot 🔥 🔥 🔥

This was quite a novelty when it was first served in 1988 for the symposium on wild chiles at the Desert Botanical Garden in Phoenix and at the Fiesta de Los Chiles at the Tucson Botanical Gardens. It is very hot in the proportions given, so some cooks may wish to reduce the quantity of chiltepins. Variations: Substitute your favorite ice cream; fruit-based ice creams and chocolate blends are particularly recommended.

$^1/_4$ cup fresh or rehydrated chiltepins, stemmed, seeded, and puréed or chiltepins en escabeche, puréed

1 gallon vanilla ice cream

Combine all ingredients and mix thoroughly until green (or red) flecks appear throughout the ice cream.

CREAMY JALAPEÑO-LIME POPSICLES

Yield: 6
Heat Scale: Medium 🔥 🔥

This recipe requires advance preparation.

$^1/_3$ cup freshly squeezed lime juice

2 cups cream

$1^1/_4$ cups granulated sugar

2 tablespoons lime zest

2 jalapeño chiles, seeds and stemmed, seeded, and minced

6 popsicle molds and sticks

In a blender, combine all ingredients and purée until smooth. Pour the mixture into 6 individual popsicle molds, insert the sticks, and freeze overnight.

PEAR AND PASILLA-CARAMEL ICE CREAM

Yield: 8 servings

Heat Scale: Mild

Yes, this is a rich dessert, but you can always substitute milk for the cream if you wish. (No, 2-percent lowfat won't work.) The pasilla chile adds a raisiny dimension that complements the pears. You will need an ice cream maker for this dessert.

- 1 dried pasilla chile, stemmed, seeded, and rehydrated in 2 cups hot water or 1 ancho
- $1^1/_2$ tablespoons unsalted butter
- $^2/_3$ cup sugar
- $3^1/_2$ cups diced ripe Bosc pears
- 4 egg yolks
- 2 cups whipping cream
- 2 tablespoons Poire Williams (clear pear brandy) or other fruit brandy (optional)

In a blender, pulse the chile and rehydrating water until chopped very fine. Strain through a sieve and reserve the pulp.

Melt the butter in a skillet over medium-low heat. Add the sugar and cook until the sugar melts and turns deep amber, stirring occasionally and breaking up any sugar lumps, about 20 minutes. Add the pears, increase the heat to medium-high, and boil until liquid thickens and pears are very tender, stirring occasionally, for about 14 minutes. Transfer the mixture to a blender and add the chile pulp.

Beat the yolks in a bowl. Bring the cream to a boil in a saucepan. Gradually whisk the hot cream into the yolks. Return the cream mixture to the saucepan. Stir over low heat until the custard thickens slightly and lightly coats the back of a spoon, about 2 minutes; do not boil. Immediately add custard to the pear mixture in the blender. Add the brandy. Blend until smooth. Cover the mixture and refrigerate until well chilled.

Process the mixture in an ice cream maker according to manufacturer's instructions. Freeze the ice cream until firm.

PEACH SUNDAES WITH CAYENNE BOURBON SAUCE

Yield: 4 servings
Heat Scale: Medium ◊ ◊

Here's a dessert with definite New Orleans overtones—bourbon, pecans, and cayenne. Only a truly daring host or hostess would serve one of the spicy ice creams in this chapter with this sauce.

1 tablespoon fresh lemon juice

3 large firm ripe peaches, peeled and pitted, thinly sliced

6 tablespoons unsalted butter

$^{1}/_{2}$ cup firmly packed light brown sugar

$^{1}/_{2}$ teaspoon cayenne powder

3 tablespoons whipping cream

$^{1}/_{2}$ cup chopped pecan pieces, toasted

1 tablespoon bourbon

1 pint vanilla ice cream

Place the lemon juice in a medium bowl. Add the peach slices and toss to coat with juice.

Melt the butter in a heavy medium saucepan over medium heat. Add brown sugar and cayenne and stir until the mixture thickens and bubbles. Add the cream 1 tablespoon at a time and stir until sugar dissolves and the sauce is thick and smooth, about 3 minutes. Stir in peaches, pecans, and bourbon. Cook until the sauce is heated through, stirring constantly, about 1 minute longer. Scoop the ice cream into bowls. Spoon the sauce over and serve.

WHITE CHOCOLATE-ANCHO CHILE ICE CREAM

Yield: 4 cups
Heat Scale: Mild

This stunning ice cream is from Suzy Dayton, former pastry chef at Santa Fe's Coyote Cafe, who served it at the Santa Fe Wine and Chile Festival in 1994.

3 dried ancho chiles, stemmed

$^1/_2$ teaspoon ground cinnamon

$^1/_4$ teaspoon ground cloves

6 ounces good-quality white chocolate, such as Tobler or Lindt

2 cups heavy cream

2 cups milk

$^3/_4$ cup granulated sugar

1 vanilla bean

6 egg yolks

4 (4-inch) cinnamon sticks for garnish

Dark semisweet chocolate shavings for garnish

Cover the chiles with hot water and let them soak until soft, about 15 minutes. Remove the chiles and discard the seeds. Place the chiles in a blender or food processor, and purée with a little of the soaking water. Stir in the cinnamon and cloves.

Melt the chocolate in a double boiler over hot water, but not boiling, water.

In a medium saucepan, combine the cream, milk, and sugar. Split the vanilla bean and scrape some of the seeds into the mixture. Bring the mixture to a boil. While whisking constantly, pour about one third of the hot milk mixture into the bowl of egg yolks. Reheat the remaining milk and return the egg yolk-milk mixture. Heat for 1 minute, whisking constantly.

Strain the mixture into a bowl. Stir in the chiles and chocolate, and chill for 15 minutes in the freezer.

Freeze in an ice cream maker according to the manufacturer's instructions. Serve garnished with a cinnamon stick and chocolate shavings.

HAWAIIAN MANGO-HABANERO-MACADAMIA ICE CREAM

Yield: 6 servings

Heat Scale: Hot

We recommend using extra-ripe mangoes for this rich, creamy dessert. You will need an ice cream maker.

2 cups whipping cream

1 cup whole milk (do not use lowfat or nonfat)

6 egg yolks

1 cup granulated sugar

2 large ripe mangoes, peeled, pitted, and diced

$^1/_2$ habanero chile, stemmed, seeded, and minced

2 teaspoons freshly squeezed lime juice

$^1/_2$ teaspoon lime zest

1 cup coarsely chopped unsalted macadamia nuts, toasted

Combine the whipping cream and milk in a saucepan and bring to a boil. Turn off the heat. Whisk the yolks and sugar together in a bowl. Gradually whisk the hot cream into the yolk mixture and return to the same saucepan. Stir over low heat until the custard thickens and will coat the spoon lightly, about 5 minutes. Immediately transfer custard to the blender. Add the mangoes and habanero and blend until smooth. Chill the custard for 1 hour in the freezer, then stir in the remaining ingredients.

Process the custard in an ice cream maker according to the manufacturer's instructions. Serve immediately or freeze the ice cream in a covered container.

ANCHO-WALNUT CREAM

Yield: 4 servings

Heat Scale: Mild

Not an ice cream per se, but rather a chilled whipped cream, this delicious dessert combines the raisiny flavor of ancho chile with toasted walnuts to create one of our favorite accompaniments to a warmed snifter of brandy.

$^1/_2$ dried ancho chile, stemmed, seeded, and
  rehydrated in 2 cups hot water

2 cups chilled whipping cream

3 tablespoons confectioners' sugar

$^1/_4$ teaspoon ground cinnamon

$1^1/_2$ tablespoons dark rum

$^3/_4$ cup finely chopped toasted walnuts

Remove the chile from the soaking water and chop finely. In a blender, combine the chile and $^1/_4$ cup soaking water and purée smooth.

Whip the cream in a medium bowl until soft peaks form. Add confectioners' sugar and rum and whip until firm peaks form. Fold in the walnuts and chile purée and mix well. Cover and chill until very cold in the refrigerator. It can also be frozen until slightly firm.

BIBLIOGRAPHY

Bacon, Josephine. *The Citrus Cookbook*. Boston: The Harvard Common Press, 1983.

Booth, George C. *The Food and Drink of Mexico*. New York: Dover, 1976.

Brillat-Savarin, Jean-Anthelme. *The Philosopher in the Kitchen*. New York: Penguin, 1981.

Bunyard, Edward. "Apples." In *The Faber Book of Food*. London: Faber and Faber, 1993.

Celebrity Kitchen. *The Fresh Fruit and Vegetable Cookbook*. New York: Berkley, 1973.

Chalmers, Irene. *The Great Food Almanac*. San Francisco: Collins Publishers, 1994.

Coady, Chantal. *Chocolate: The Food of the Gods*. San Francisco: Chronicle Books, 1993.

Cranwell, John Philips. *The Hellfire Cookbook*. New York: Quadrangle, 1975.

David, Elizabeth. *Summer Cooking*. New York: Penguin, 1965.

Elkort, Michael. *The Secret Life of Food*. California: Tarcher, 1991.

Fisher, M.F.K. *The Art of Eating*. New York: Collier Books, 1990.

Hayot, Roger. *Dinner at the Authentic Cafe*. New York: Macmillan, 1995.

Herbst, Sharon Tyler. *The Food Lover's Tiptionary*. New York: Hearst Books, 1994.

Hillman, Howard. *Kitchen Science*. Boston: Houghton Mifflin, 1981.

Hutson, Lucinda. *Tequila!* Berkeley, CA: Ten Speed Press, 1995.

Katz, Samantha. *Fabulous Food*. Florida: Globe Communications, 1994.

Kuhn, Loni. "The Complete Guild to the Pleasures of Preserving." *Bon Appetit*, 79, Sept., 1982.

Makay, Ian. *Food For Thought*. Freedom, CA: Crossing Press, 1995.

McGee, Harold. *On Food and Cooking.* New York: Charles Scribner's Sons, 1984.Nusom, Lynn. *Spoon Desserts.* Freedom, CA: Crossing Press, 1990.

Pozel, Lynda A. "Jams That Sizzle." *Chile Pepper,* Jan./Feb. 1996.

Prescott, William H. *History of the Conquest of Mexico.* Chicago: University of Chicago Press, 1966.

Ray, Richard and Lance Walheim. *Citrus.* Los Angeles: Price Stern Sloan, 1980.

Richardson, Dr. Mabel W. *Tropical Fruit Recipes.* Miami, FL: The Rare Fruit Council International, 1976.

Roden, Claudia. *A Book of Middle Eastern Foods.* New York: Vintage Books, 1974.

Root, Waverly. *Food.* New York: Simon and Schuster, 1980.

Schneider, Elizabeth. "Where the Chocolate Tree Blooms." *Saveur,* 96, Sept./Oct. 1995.

Schumann, Charles. *Tropical Bar Book.* New York: Stewart, Tabori & Chang, 1989.

Spencer, Colin and Clifton, Claire. *The Faber Book of Food.* London: Faber, 1993.

Stashower, Daniel. "Original Oxford Marmalade." *Eating Well,* 49, Jan./Feb. 1994.

Stern, Jane and Michael. *American Gourmet.* New York: HarperCollins, 1991.

Tannahill, Reay. *Food In History.* New York: Crown, 1988.

Tobias, Doris and Mary Merris. *The Golden Lemon.* New York: Atheneum, 1978.

Tousssaint-Samat, Maguelonne. *History of Food.* Cambridge, MA: Blackwell Publishers, 1992.

Trollope, Frances. "Water Melons." In *The Faber Book of Food.* London: Faber and Faber, 1993.

Van Aken, Norman. The Great Exotic Fruit Book. Berkeley, CA: Ten Speed Press, 1995.

Visser, Margaret. *Much Depends on Dinner.* New York: Grove Press, 1986.

Weil, Andrew. *The Marriage of the Sun and Moon.* Boston: Houghton Mifflin, 1980.

MAIL-ORDER SOURCES & RETAIL SHOPS

▲▲▲▲▲▲▲▲▲▲▲▲▲▲▲▲▲▲▲▲▲▲▲▲▲▲▲▲▲▲▲▲▲▲▲▲

MAIL-ORDER CATALOGS

Here are the main mail-order suppliers of chile-related products.

Blazing Chile Bros.
(800) 473-9040

Chile Pepper Magazine
P.O. Box 80780
Albuquerque, NM 87198
(800) 359-1483

Chile Today-Hot Tamale
919 Highway 33, Suite 47
Freehold, NJ 07728
(908) 308-1151

Colorado Spice Company
5030 Nome Street, Unit A
Denver, CO 80239
(303) 373-0141

Coyote Cocina
1364 Rufina Circle #1
Santa Fe, NM 87501
(800) 866-HOWL

Dean and DeLuca
Mail Order Department
560 Broadway
New York, NY 10012
(212) 431-1691

Don Alfonso Foods
P.O. Box 201988
Austin, TX 78720
(800) 456-6100

Enchanted Seeds
P.O. Box 6087
Las Cruces, NM 88006
(505) 233-3033

Flamingo Flats
Box 441
St. Michael's, MD 21663
(800) 468-8841

Frieda's, Inc.
P.O. Box 584888
Los Angeles, CA 90058
(800) 421-9477

GMB Specialty Foods, Inc.
P.O. Box 962
San Juan Capistrano, CA
92693-0962
(714) 240-3053

Hot Sauce Club of America
P.O. Box 687
Indian Rocks Beach, FL
34635-0687
(800) Sauce-2-U

Hot Sauce Harry's
The Dallas Farmer's Market
3422 Flair Drive
Dallas, TX 75229
(214) 902-8552

Le Saucier
Faneuil Hall Marketplace
Boston, MA 02109
(617) 227-9649

Lotta Hotta
7895 Mastin
Overland Park, KS 66204
(800) LOTT-HOT

Melissa's World Variety Produce
P.O. Box 21127
Los Angeles, CA 90021
(800) 468-7111

Mo Hotta, Mo Betta
P.O. Box 4136
San Luis Obispo, CA 93403
(800) 462-3220

Nancy's Specialty Market
P.O. Box 327
Wye Mills, MD 21679
(800) 462-6291

Old Southwest Trading Co.
P.O. Box 7545
Albuquerque, NM 87194
(505) 836-0168

Pendery's
304 East Belknap
Fort Worth, TX 76102
(800) 533-1879

Pepper Gal
P.O. Box 23006
Ft. Lauderdale, FL 33307
(305) 537-5540

Pepper Joe's, Inc.
7 Tyburn Court
Timonium, MD 21093
(410) 561-8158

Santa Fe School of Cooking
116 W. San Francisco Street
Santa Fe, NM 87501
(505) 983-4511

Shepherd Garden Seeds
6116 Highway 9
Felton, CA 95018
(408) 335-6910

South Side Pepper Co.
320 N. Walnut St.
Mechanicsburg, PA 17055

RETAIL SHOPS

Here are the retail shops or markets that specialize in hot and spicy products. Some of them have mail-order catalogs. It has been difficult to keep up with the number of new hot shop retailers, so we apologize in advance if we have overlooked any.

WEST

Central Market
4001 N. Lamar
Austin, TX 78756
(512) 206-1000

Chile Pepper Mania
1709-F Airline Highway
P.O. Box 232
Hollister, CA 95023
(408) 636-8259

Colorado Spice Company
5030 Nome Street, Unit A
Denver, CO 80239
(800) 67-SPICE

Eagle Mountain Gifts
634 S. China Lake Boulevard
Ridgecrest, CA 93555
(619) 375-3071

GMB Specialty Foods, Inc.
28075 Via Rueda
San Juan Capistrano, CA 92675
(714) 240-3053

Hot Hot Hot
56 South Delacey Avenue
Pasadena, CA 91105
(818) 564-1090

Hot Stuff
288 Argonne Avenue
Long Beach, CA 90803
(310) 438-1118

Hots for You-Chile Pepper
Emporium
8843 Shady Meadow Drive
Sandy, UT 84093
(801) 255-7800

Jones and Bones
621 Capitola Avenue
Capitola, CA 95010
(408) 462-0521

The Original Hot Sauce Company
Avenue of Shops
1421-C Larimer Street
Denver, CO 80202
(303) 615-5812

Rivera's Chile Shop
109¹/₂ Concho Street
San Antonio, TX 78207
(210) 226-9106

Salsas, Etc.!
3683 Tunis Avenue
San Jose, CA 95132
(408) 263-6392

Salsas, Etc.
374 Eastridge Mall
San Jose, CA 95122
(408) 223-9020

Sambet's Cajun Store
8644 Spicewood Springs Road, Suite F
Austin, TX 78759
(800) 472-6238

Sherwood's Lotsa Hotsa
948 Main Street
Ramona, CA 92065
(619) 443-7982

Some Like It Hot
3208 Scott Street
San Francisco, CA 94123
(415) 441-7HOT

The Stonewall Chili Pepper Company
Highway 290 East
P.O. Box 241
Stonewall, TX 78671
(210) 644-2667
(800) 232-2995

Uncle Bill's House of Hot Sauce
311 N. Higgins Avenue
Missoula, MT 59801
(406) 543-5627

The Whole Earth Grainery
111 Ivinson Avenue
Laramie, WY 82070
(307) 745-4268

Chile Hill Emporium
Highway 44 at the Rio Grande
Box 9100
Bernalillo, NM 87004
(505) 867-3294

The Chile Shop
109 East Water Street
Santa Fe, NM 87501
(505) 983-6080

Chile Patch U.S.A.
204 San Felipe NW
Albuquerque, NM 87104
(505) 242-4454
(800) 458-0646
Chili Pepper Emporium
328 San Felipe NW
Albuquerque NM 87104
(505) 242-7538

Coyote Cafe General Store
132 West Water Street
Santa Fe, NM 87501
(505) 982-2454
(800) 866-HOWL

Free Spirit
420 S. Mill Avenue
Tempe, AZ 85281
(602) 966-4339

Garden Gate Gift Shop
Tucson Botonical Gardens
2150 North Alvernon Way
Tucson, AZ 85712
(602) 326-9686

Gourmet Gallery
320 N. Highway 89A
Singua Plaza
Sedona, AZ 86336

Hatch Chile Express
622 Franklin Street
P.O. Box 350
Hatch, NM 87937
(505) 267-3226

Potpourri
303 Romero NW
Plaza Don Luis, Old Town
Albuquerque, NM 87104
(505) 243-4087

Santa Fe Emporium
104 W. San Francisco
Santa Fe, NM 87501
(505) 984-1966

Santa Fe School of Cooking
116 West San Francisco Street
Santa Fe, NM 87501
(505) 983-4511

Senor Chile's at Rawhide
23020 North Scottsdale Road
Scottsdale, AZ 85255
(602) 563-5600

MIDWEST

Calido Chile Traders
5360 Merriam Drive
Merriam, KS 66203
(800) 568-8468

Chutneys
143 Delaware Street
Lexington, OH 44904
(419) 884-2853

Hot Kicks
4349 Raymir Place
Wauwatosa, WI 53222
(414) 536-7808

The Hot Spot
1 Riverfront Plaza #300
Lawrence, KS 66044
(913) 841-7200

Lotta Hotta
3150 Mercier, Suite 516
Kansas City, MO 64111
1-800-LOTT-HOT

SOUTH

Caribbean Spice Company
2 S. Church Street
Fairhope, AL 36532
(800) 990-6088

Dat'l Do-It Hot Shop
106 Saint George Street
P.O. Box 4019
St. Augustine, FL 32085
(904) 824-5303
(800) HOT-DATL

Dat'l Do-It Hot Shop
Dadeland Mall
7535 North Kendall Drive
Miami, FL 37211
(305) 253-0248

Fiery Foods
909 20th Avenue South
Nashville, TN 37212
(615) 320-5475

Hot Licks
P.O. Box 7854
Hollywood, FL 33081
(305) 987-7105

The Hot Spot
5777 South Lakeshore Drive
Shreveport, LA 71119
(318) 635-3581

New Orleans School of Cooking
620 Decatur Street
New Orleans, LA 70130
(504) 482-3632

Tabasco Country Store
Avery Island, LA 70513
(318) 365-8173

Tabasco Country Store
Riverwalk Marketplace
1 Poydras Street
New Orleans, LA 70130
(504) 523-1711

MID-ATLANTIC

Peppers
2009 Highway 1
Dewey Beach, DE 19971
(302) 227-1958
(800) 998-3473

Pepperhead Hot Shoppe
7036 Kristi Court
Garner, NC 27529
(919) 553-4576

Pepper Joe's, Inc.
7 Tyburn Court
Timonium, MD 21093
(410) 561-8158

Some Like It Hot
301 S. Light Street
Harbor Place
Baltimore, MD 21202
(410) 547-2HOT

NORTHEAST

Hell's Kitchen
216 Lipincott Avenue
Riverside, NJ 08075
(609) 764-1487

Hell's Kitchen
Pennsasken Mart-Store #328
Rt. #130
Pennasken, NJ 08019
(609) 764-1330

Hot Papa's Fiery Flavors
11121 Weeden Road
Randolph, NY 14772
(716) 358-4302

Hot Stuff
227 Sullivan Street
New York, NY 10012
(212) 254-6120
(800) 466-8206

Le Saucier
Faneiul Hall Marketplace
Boston, MA 02109
(617) 227-9649

Pungent Pod
25 Haviland Road
Queensbury, NY 12804
(518) 793-3180

Santa Fe Trading Company
7 Main Street
Tarrytown, NY 10591
(914) 332-1730

CANADA

Hot Lovers Fiery Foods
1282 Wolseley Avenue
Winnipeg, Manitoba R3G IH4
(204) 772-6418

CARIBBEAN

Down Island Ventures
P.O. Box 37
Cruz Bay, St. John
U.S. Virgin Islands
(809) 693-7000

Pampered Pirate
4 Norre Gade
St. Thomas
U.S. Virgin Islands 00802
(809) 775-5450

INDEX

▲▲▲

MORE HOT STUFF FROM TEN SPEED PRESS

THE FIERY CUISINES

by Dave DeWitt and Nancy Gerlach

"DeWitt and Gerlach seem to know everything about 'firepower' and present fine international samplings of hot and spicy dishes."
—*Booklist*

This is a comprehensive guide to the world's most delicious hot dishes. Includes nearly 200 recipes for appetizers, condiments, soups, salads, breads, and main dishes, as well as the history of hot spices. 229 pages

THE HABANERO COOKBOOK

by Dave DeWitt and Nancy Gerlach

More than 100 recipes devoted to the world's hottest pepper are collected here, as well as a fascinating history of the habanero's traditional and contemporary use in Caribbean, South America, and Central American cuisine. 160 pages

THE PEPPER GARDEN

by Dave DeWitt and Paul W. Bosland

The complete guide to growing your own chile peppers, whether you live in pepper-growing country or other regions. DeWitt and Bosland (one of the foremost chile pepper breeders and associate professor of horticulture at New Mexico State) offer everything you need to know to grow and enjoy peppers, including variety selection tips, planting and cultivation information, and harvesting directions. 240 pages

THE GREAT CHILE BOOK

by Mark Miller with John Harrisson

A full-color photographic guide to one hundred varieties of chiles—fifty each of fresh and dried, including a brief description, tips for use, and a heat rating. The book also gives a history of the chile in Mexican and Southwestern tradition, and recipes from the Coyote Cafe. 128 pages

CHILE PEPPER POSTERS

Created by Mark Miller of the Coyote Cafe, these sumptuous chile identification posters show thirty-one fresh chiles and thirty-five dried ones, with heat ratings and cooking tips for each. With their unique pre-Colombian borders and vivid photography, these framing-quality prints make a fabulous addition to any wall.

For more information, or to order, call us at the number below. We accept VISA, Mastercard, and American Express. You may also wish to write for our free catalog of over 500 books, posters, and audiotapes.

TEN SPEED PRESS
P.O. Box 7123
Berkeley, CA 94707
800/841-BOOK